CROCK·POT

◆ THE ORIGINAL SLOW COOKER ◆

Busy Family *Recipes*

Publications International, Ltd.

Photography on pages 11, 15, 33, 35, 36, 37, 39, 40, 41, 57, 59, 60, 61, 63, 71, 81, 85, 87, 91, 94, 96, 99, 101 and 165 by Chris Cassidy Photography.
Photographers: Chris Cassidy
Photographer's Assistant: Kari Lane McCluskey
Prop Stylist: Nancy Natow-Cassidy
Food Stylists: Josephine Orba, Carol Smoller and Cindy Whelan
Assistant Food Stylist: Sheila Grannon

Pictured on the front cover: Smoked Sausage and Navy Bean Soup *(page 126).*
Pictured on the back cover (clockwise from top): No More "Chili" Nights *(page 12),* Easy Beef Stew *(page 69)* and Meatballs and Spaghetti Sauce *(page 144).*

ISBN-13: 978-1-60553-184-7
ISBN-10: 1-60553-184-7

Library of Congress Control Number: 2009938812

Manufactured in China.

8 7 6 5 4 3 2 1

TABLE OF CONTENTS

Slow Cooker Hints and Tips

Slow Cooker Sizes

Smaller slow cookers—such as 1- to 3½-quart models—are the perfect size for cooking for singles, a couple, or empty-nesters (and also for serving dips).

While medium-size slow cookers (those holding somewhere between 3 quarts and 5 quarts) will easily cook enough food at a time to feed a small family, they're also convenient for holiday side dishes or appetizers.

Large slow cookers are great for large family dinners, holiday entertaining, and potluck suppers. A 6-quart to 7-quart model is ideal if you like to make meals in advance, or have dinner tonight and store leftovers for another day.

Types of Slow Cookers

Current **CROCK-POT®** slow cookers come equipped with many different features and benefits, from auto cook programs to stovetop-safe stoneware to timed programming. Visit **www.crockpot.com** to find the slow cooker that best suits your needs.

How you plan to use a slow cooker may affect the model you choose to purchase. For everyday cooking, choose a size large enough to serve your family. If you plan to use the slow cooker primarily for entertaining, choose one of the larger sizes. Basic slow cookers can hold as little as 16 ounces or as much as 7 quarts. The smallest sizes are great for keeping dips hot on a buffet, while the larger sizes can more readily fit large quantities of food and larger roasts.

Cooking, Stirring, and Food Safety

CROCK-POT® slow cookers are safe to leave unattended. The outer heating base may get hot as it cooks, but it should not pose a fire hazard. The heating element in the heating base functions at a low wattage and is safe for your countertops.

Your slow cooker should be filled about one-half to three-fourths full for most recipes unless otherwise instructed. Lean meats such as chicken or pork tenderloin will cook faster than meats with more connective tissue and fat such as beef chuck or pork shoulder. Bone-in meats will take longer than boneless cuts. Typical slow cooker dishes take approximately 7 to 8 hours to reach the simmer point on LOW and about 3 to 4 hours on HIGH. Once the vegetables and meat start to simmer and braise, their flavors will fully blend and meat will become fall-off-the-bone tender.

According to the USDA, all bacteria are killed at a temperature of 165°F. It is important to follow the recommended cooking times and not to open the lid often, especially early in the cooking process when heat is building up inside the unit. If you need to open the lid to check on your food or are adding additional ingredients, remember to allow additional cooking time if necessary to ensure food is cooked through and tender.

Large slow cookers, the 6- to 7-quart sizes, may benefit with a quick stir halfway during cook time to help distribute heat and promote even cooking. It's usually unnecessary to stir at all, as even ½ cup liquid will help to distribute heat and the crockery is the perfect medium for holding food at an even temperature throughout the cooking process.

Oven-Safe

All **CROCK-POT**® slow cooker removable crockery inserts may (without their lids) be used safely in ovens at up to 400°F. Also, all **CROCK-POT**® slow cookers are microwavable without their

lids. If you own another brand slow cooker, please refer to your owner's manual for specific crockery cooking medium tolerances.

Frozen Food

Frozen food or partially frozen food can be successfully cooked in a slow cooker; however, it will require longer cooking than the same recipe made with fresh food. It's almost always preferable to thaw frozen food prior to placing it in the slow cooker. Using an instant-read thermometer is recommended to ensure meat is fully cooked through.

Pasta and Rice

If you're converting a recipe that calls for uncooked pasta, cook the pasta on the stovetop just until slightly tender before adding to slow cooker. If you are converting a recipe that calls for cooked rice, stir in raw rice with other ingredients; add ¼ cup extra liquid per ¼ cup of raw rice.

Beans

Beans must be softened completely

before combining with sugar and/or acidic foods. Sugar and acid have a hardening effect on beans and will prevent softening. Fully cooked canned beans may be used as a substitute for dried beans.

Vegetables

Root vegetables often cook more slowly than meat. Cut vegetables accordingly to cook at the same rate as meat—large or small, or lean versus marbled—and place near the sides or bottom of the stoneware to facilitate cooking.

Herbs

Fresh herbs add flavor and color when added at the end of the cooking cycle; if added at the beginning, many fresh herbs' flavor will dissipate over long cook times. Ground and/or dried herbs and spices work well in slow cooking and may be added at the beginning, and for dishes with shorter cook times, hearty fresh herbs such as rosemary and thyme hold up well. The flavor power of all herbs and spices can vary greatly depending on their particular strength and shelf life. Use chili powders and garlic powder sparingly, as these can sometimes intensify over the long cook times. Always taste dish at end of cook cycle and correct seasonings including salt and pepper.

Liquids

It is not necessary to use more than ½ to 1 cup liquid in most instances since juices in meats and vegetables are retained more in slow cooking than in conventional cooking. Excess liquid can be cooked down and concentrated after slow cooking on the stovetop or by removing meat and vegetables from stoneware, stirring in one of the following thickeners, and setting the slow cooker to HIGH. Cook on HIGH for approximately 15 minutes until juices are thickened.

Flour: All-purpose flour is often used to thicken soups or stews. Place flour in a small bowl or cup and stir in enough cold water to make a thin, lump-free mixture. With the slow cooker on HIGH, quickly stir the flour mixture into the liquid in the slow cooker. Cook, stirring frequently, until the mixture thickens.

Cornstarch: Cornstarch gives sauces a clear, shiny appearance; it is used most often for sweet dessert sauces and stir-fry sauces. Place cornstarch in a small bowl or cup and stir in cold water, stirring until the cornstarch dissolves. Quickly stir this mixture into the liquid in the slow cooker; the sauce will thicken as soon as the liquid boils. Cornstarch breaks down with too much heat, so never add it at the beginning of the slow cooking process, and turn off the heat as soon as the sauce thickens.

Arrowroot: Arrowroot (or arrowroot flour) comes from the root of a tropical plant that is dried and ground to a powder; it produces a thick clear sauce. Those who are allergic to wheat often use it in place of flour. Place arrowroot in a small bowl or cup and stir in cold water until the mixture is smooth. Quickly stir this mixture into the liquid in the slow cooker. Arrowroot thickens below the boiling point, so it even works well in a slow cooker on LOW. Too much stirring can break down an arrowroot mixture.

Tapioca: Tapioca is a starchy substance extracted from the root of the cassava plant. Its greatest advantage is that it withstands long cooking, making it an ideal choice for slow cooking. Add it at the beginning of cooking and you'll get a clear thickened sauce in the finished dish. Dishes using tapioca as a thickener are best cooked on the LOW setting; tapioca may become stringy when boiled for a long time.

Milk

Milk, cream, and sour cream break down during extended cooking. When possible, add during last 15 to 30 minutes of cooking, until just heated through. Condensed soups may be substituted for milk and can cook for extended times.

Fish

Fish is delicate and should be stirred in gently during the last 15 to 30 minutes of cooking time. Cook until just cooked through and serve immediately.

Baked Goods

If you wish to prepare bread, cakes, or pudding cakes in a slow cooker, you may want to purchase a covered, vented metal cake pan accessory for your slow cooker. You can also use any straight-sided soufflé dish or deep cake pan that will fit into the ceramic insert of your unit. Baked goods can be prepared directly in the insert; however, they can be a little difficult to remove from the insert, so follow the recipe directions carefully.

SLOW COOKER CLASSICS

Your family is bound to find new favorites among
these classic slow cooker recipes including
delicious main dishes and sumptuous sides

baked beans

 2 cans (16 ounces each) baked beans
 1 cup ketchup
 ½ cup barbecue sauce
 ½ cup packed brown sugar
 5 slices bacon, chopped
 ½ green bell pepper, chopped
 ½ onion, chopped
 1½ teaspoons prepared mustard
 Fresh parsley (optional)

Place all ingredients in **CROCK-POT®** slow cooker. Stir well to combine. Cover; cook
on LOW 8 to 12 hours or on HIGH 3 to 4 hours. Garnish with fresh parsley, if desired.

Makes 6 to 8 servings

honey-glazed chicken wings

. . . .

- 3 tablespoons vegetable oil, divided
- 3 pounds chicken wings, tips removed
- 1 cup honey
- ½ cup soy sauce
- 1 clove garlic, minced
- 2 tablespoons tomato paste
- 2 teaspoons water
- 1 teaspoon sugar
- 1 teaspoon black pepper

. . . .

1. Heat 1½ tablespoons oil in skillet over medium heat until hot. Brown chicken wings on each side in batches to prevent crowding. Turn each piece as it browns, about 1 to 2 minutes per side. Transfer with slotted spoon to **CROCK-POT®** slow cooker.

2. Combine honey, soy sauce, remaining 1½ tablespoons vegetable oil and garlic in medium bowl. Whisk in tomato paste, water, sugar and pepper. Pour sauce over chicken. Cover; cook on LOW 6 to 8 hours or on HIGH 3 to 4 hours.

Makes 6 to 8 servings

no more "chili" nights

. . . .

1½ pounds lean ground beef

1 small onion, chopped

2 cans (15½ ounces each) red kidney beans, rinsed and drained

1 can (29 ounces) tomato sauce

1 can (14½ ounces) diced tomatoes with green peppers, celery and onions, undrained

1 can (14½ ounces) diced tomatoes and onions, undrained

1 can water (use 14½-ounce can to measure)

1 can (10 ounces) diced tomatoes and green chilies, undrained

½ green bell pepper, cored, seeded and chopped, plus additional for garnish

3 tablespoons chili powder

2 tablespoons sugar

2 teaspoons salt

1 teaspoon minced garlic or 2 cloves fresh garlic

1 teaspoon Worcestershire sauce

1 teaspoon black pepper

1 teaspoon ground cumin

Shredded cheese (optional)

Crackers (optional)

. . . .

1. Brown ground beef and onion 6 to 8 minutes in large skillet over medium-high heat, stirring to break up meat. Drain and discard excess fat. Transfer meat mixture to **CROCK-POT**® slow cooker.

2. Add remaining ingredients. Stir well to combine. Cover; cook on LOW 8 to 10 hours. Garnish with cheese and bell pepper, and serve with crackers, if desired.

Makes 4 to 6 servings

maple-glazed meatballs

- 1½ cups ketchup
- 1 cup maple syrup or maple-flavored syrup
- ⅓ cup reduced-sodium soy sauce
- 1 tablespoon quick-cooking tapioca
- 1½ teaspoons ground allspice
- 1 teaspoon dry mustard
- 2 packages (about 16 ounces each) frozen fully cooked meatballs, partially thawed and separated
- 1 can (20 ounces) pineapple chunks in juice, drained

1. Combine ketchup, maple syrup, soy sauce, tapioca, allspice and mustard in **CROCK-POT®** slow cooker.

2. Carefully stir meatballs and pineapple chunks into ketchup mixture.

3. Cover; cook on LOW 5 to 6 hours. Stir before serving. Serve warm; insert cocktail picks, if desired.

Makes about 48 meatballs

tip

For a quick main dish, serve meatballs over hot cooked rice.

rustic garlic mashed potatoes

- 2 pounds baking potatoes, unpeeled and cut into ½-inch cubes
- ¼ cup water
- 2 tablespoons butter, cut into ⅛-inch pieces
- 1½ teaspoons salt
- ½ teaspoon garlic powder
- ¼ teaspoon black pepper
- 1 cup milk

Place all ingredients except milk in **CROCK-POT**® slow cooker; toss to combine. Cover; cook on LOW 7 hours or on HIGH 4 hours. Add milk to potatoes. Mash potatoes with potato masher or electric mixer until smooth.

Makes 5 servings

jambalaya

- 1 can (28 ounces) whole tomatoes, undrained
- 1 pound cooked andouille sausage, sliced*
- 2 cups boiled ham, diced
- 2 cups water
- 1 cup uncooked rice
- 2 onions, chopped
- 2 stalks celery, sliced
- ½ green bell pepper, diced
- ¼ cup tomato paste
- 2 tablespoons olive or canola oil
- 1 tablespoon minced garlic
- 1 tablespoon minced flat-leaf parsley
- 1 to 2 teaspoons hot pepper sauce, to taste
- ½ teaspoon dried thyme
- 2 whole cloves
- 1 pound medium to large shrimp, peeled, deveined and cleaned

*Or, substitute 1 pound cooked smoked sausage or kielbasa.

1. Place all ingredients except shrimp in **CROCK-POT**® slow cooker. Stir well to combine. Cover; cook on LOW 8 to 10 hours or on HIGH 4 to 6 hours.

2. Thirty minutes before serving, turn **CROCK-POT**® slow cooker to HIGH. Add shrimp and continue cooking until shrimp are done. Adjust seasonings, as desired.

Makes 6 to 8 servings

lemon-mint red potatoes

- 2 pounds new red potatoes
- 3 tablespoons extra-virgin olive oil
- ¾ teaspoon dried Greek seasoning or dried oregano leaves
- ¼ teaspoon garlic powder
- 1 teaspoon salt
- ¼ teaspoon black pepper
- 2 tablespoons lemon juice
- 1 teaspoon grated lemon peel
- 2 tablespoons butter
- ¼ cup chopped fresh mint leaves, divided

1. Coat inside of **CROCK-POT®** slow cooker with nonstick cooking spray. Add potatoes and oil, stirring gently to coat. Sprinkle with Greek seasoning, garlic powder, salt and pepper. Cover and cook on LOW 7 hours or on HIGH 4 hours.

2. Stir in lemon juice, lemon peel, butter and 2 tablespoons mint. Stir until butter is completely melted. Cover and cook 15 minutes to allow flavors to blend. Sprinkle with remaining mint.

Makes 4 servings

tip

It's easy to prepare this recipe ahead of time; simply follow instructions as listed and then turn off heat and let stand at room temperature for up to 2 hours. Reheat or serve at room temperature.

old-fashioned split pea soup

- 4 quarts chicken broth
- 2 pounds dried split peas
- 1 cup chopped ham
- ½ cup chopped onion
- ½ cup chopped celery
- 2 teaspoons salt
- 2 teaspoons black pepper

1. Place all ingredients in **CROCK-POT®** slow cooker. Stir well to combine. Cover; cook on LOW 8 to 10 hours or on HIGH 4 to 6 hours, or until peas are soft.

2. Mix with hand mixer or hand blender on LOW speed until smooth.

Makes 8 servings

beef bourguignon

- 6 strips bacon, cut into 1- to 2-inch pieces
- 3 pounds beef rump roast, cut into 1-inch cubes
- 1 large carrot, peeled and sliced
- 1 medium onion, sliced
- 1 teaspoon salt
- ½ teaspoon black pepper
- 3 tablespoons all-purpose flour
- 1 can (10 ounces) condensed beef broth
- 2 cups red or Burgundy wine
- 1 pound fresh mushrooms, sliced
- ½ pound small white onions, peeled
- 1 tablespoon tomato paste
- 2 cloves garlic, minced
- ½ teaspoon dried thyme
- 1 whole bay leaf

1. Cook bacon in skillet over medium heat until crisp. Remove; set aside.

2. Add beef to skillet and brown well. Remove; set aside.

3. Brown carrot and onion in skillet. Transfer to **CROCK-POT**® slow cooker. Season with salt and pepper. Stir in flour, add broth and mix well. Stir in beef and bacon.

4. Add wine, mushrooms, onions, tomato paste, garlic, thyme and bay leaf. Cover; cook on LOW 10 to 12 hours or HIGH 5 to 6 hours.

Makes 6 to 8 servings

herbed fall vegetables

- 2 medium Yukon gold potatoes, peeled and cut into ½-inch dice
- 2 medium sweet potatoes, peeled and cut into ½-inch dice
- 3 parsnips, peeled and cut into ½-inch dice
- 1 medium head of fennel, sliced and cut into ½-inch dice
- ½ to ¾ cup chopped fresh herbs, such as tarragon, parsley, sage or thyme
- ¼ cup (½ stick) butter, cut into small pieces
- 1 cup chicken broth
- 1 tablespoon Dijon mustard
- 1 tablespoon salt

  Freshly ground black pepper, to taste

1. Combine potatoes, parsnips, fennel, herbs and butter in **CROCK-POT®** slow cooker.

2. Whisk together broth, mustard, salt and pepper in small bowl. Pour mixture over vegetables. Cover; cook on LOW 4½ hours or on HIGH 3 hours or until vegetables are tender, stirring occasionally to ensure even cooking.

Makes 6 servings

chicken soup

- 6 cups chicken broth
- 1½ pounds boneless, skinless chicken breasts, cubed
- 2 cups sliced carrots
- 1 cup sliced mushrooms
- 1 red bell pepper, chopped
- 1 onion, chopped
- 2 tablespoons grated fresh ginger
- 3 teaspoons minced garlic
- ½ teaspoon crushed red pepper

Salt and black pepper, to taste

Place all ingredients in **CROCK-POT®** slow cooker. Cover; cook on LOW 6 to 7 hours or on HIGH 3 to 3½ hours.

Makes 4 to 6 servings

caramelized french onion soup

- 4 extra-large sweet onions, peeled
- ¼ cup (½ stick) butter
- 2 cups dry white wine
- 8 cups beef or vegetable broth, divided
- 2 cups water
- 1 tablespoon minced fresh thyme
- 6 slices French bread, toasted
- 1 cup shredded Swiss or Gruyère cheese

1. Cut each onion into quarters. Cut each quarter into ¼-inch-thick slices. Heat skillet over medium heat until hot. Add butter and onions. Cook until soft and caramel brown, about 45 to 50 minutes, stirring every 7 to 8 minutes. Transfer to **CROCK-POT®** slow cooker.

2. Add wine to skillet and let liquid reduce to about ½ cup, simmering about 15 minutes. Transfer to **CROCK-POT®** slow cooker.

3. Add broth, water and thyme to **CROCK-POT®** slow cooker. Cover; cook on HIGH 2½ hours or until thoroughly heated.

4. To serve, ladle soup into individual ovenproof soup bowls. Float one slice of toast in each bowl and sprinkle with cheese. Preheat oven broiler and place bowls on top shelf of oven. Broil 3 to 5 minutes, or until cheese is melted and golden. Serve immediately.

Makes 6 servings

campfired-up sloppy joes

- 1½ pounds lean ground beef
- ½ cup chopped sweet onion
- 1 medium red bell pepper, cored, seeded and chopped
- 1 large clove garlic, minced
- ½ cup ketchup
- ½ cup barbecue sauce
- 2 tablespoons cider vinegar
- 1 tablespoon Worcestershire sauce
- 1 tablespoon packed brown sugar
- 1 teaspoon chili powder
- 1 can (8 ounces) baked beans
- 6 kaiser rolls, split and warmed

  Shredded sharp Cheddar cheese (optional)

serving suggestion

Serve with a side of coleslaw.

1. Brown ground beef, onion, bell pepper and garlic 6 to 8 minutes in large skillet over medium-high heat, stirring to break up meat. Drain and discard excess fat. Transfer beef mixture to **CROCK-POT®** slow cooker.

2. Combine ketchup, barbecue sauce, vinegar, Worcestershire sauce, brown sugar and chili powder in small bowl. Transfer to **CROCK-POT®** slow cooker.

3. Add baked beans. Stir well to combine. Cover; cook on HIGH 3 hours.

4. To serve, place ½ cup sloppy joe mixture on bottom halves of rolls. Sprinkle with Cheddar cheese, if desired, before covering with roll tops.

Makes 4 to 6 servings

traditional cassoulet

- 1 small onion, finely chopped
- 2 cloves garlic, finely chopped
- ½ cup finely chopped, peeled carrots
- ½ cup roughly chopped, seeded tomatoes
- 1 can (about 15 ounces) cannellini beans, rinsed and drained
- ¼ cup bread crumbs
- 2 tablespoons finely chopped fresh marjoram leaves
- 2 tablespoons finely chopped fresh parsley leaves
- 2 tablespoons olive oil
- 1½ pounds chicken thighs
- ½ pound bulk pork sausage
- ½ cup dry white wine
- ½ cup chicken broth

1. Combine onion, garlic, carrots, tomatoes, beans, bread crumbs and fresh herbs in **CROCK-POT®** slow cooker. Set aside.

2. Heat olive oil in large skillet over medium-high heat. Add chicken (in batches, if necessary) and cook 3 to 4 minutes per side or until brown. Place chicken on top of mixture in slow cooker. Add sausage to skillet. Cook, stirring to break up meat, until cooked through. Transfer sausage to slow cooker with slotted spoon.

3. Return skillet to medium-high heat. Add wine and chicken broth to skillet and stir to scrape up any browned bits. Bring to a boil and cook until liquid is reduced to about one third its original volume. Remove from heat.

4. Pour reduced liquid over contents of slow cooker. Cover and cook on LOW 6 to 7 hours or on HIGH 3½ hours.

Makes 4 servings

old-fashioned sauerkraut

- 8 slices bacon, chopped
- 2 pounds sauerkraut
- 1 large head cabbage or 2 small heads
- 2½ cups chopped onions
- ¼ cup (½ stick) butter
- 2 tablespoons sugar
- 1 teaspoon salt
- 1 teaspoon black pepper

note

Add your favorite bratwurst, knockwurst or other sausage to this recipe to make an entire meal.

1. Heat skillet over medium heat until hot. Cook and stir bacon until crisp. Remove skillet from heat and set aside. (Do not drain bacon fat.)

2. Place sauerkraut, cabbage, onions, butter, sugar, salt and pepper in **CROCK-POT®** slow cooker. Pour bacon and bacon fat over sauerkraut mixture. Cover; cook on LOW 4 to 5 hours or on HIGH 1 to 3 hours.

Makes 8 to 10 servings

classic beef and noodles

- 1 tablespoon vegetable oil
- 2 pounds beef for stew, cut into 1-inch pieces
- ¼ pound fresh mushrooms, sliced into halves
- 2 tablespoons chopped onion
- 2 cloves garlic, minced
- 1 teaspoon salt
- 1 teaspoon dried oregano
- ½ teaspoon black pepper
- ¼ teaspoon dried marjoram
- 1 bay leaf
- 1½ cups beef broth
- ⅓ cup dry sherry
- 1 container (8 ounces) sour cream
- ½ cup all-purpose flour
- ¼ cup water
- 4 cups hot cooked noodles

1. Heat oil in large skillet over medium heat until hot. Brown beef on all sides. (Work in batches, if necessary.) Drain fat and discard.

2. Combine beef, mushrooms, onion, garlic, salt, oregano, pepper, marjoram and bay leaf in **CROCK-POT**® slow cooker. Pour in broth and sherry. Cover; cook on LOW 8 to 10 hours or on HIGH 4 to 5 hours. Remove bay leaf and discard.

3. Combine sour cream, flour and water in small bowl. Stir about 1 cup cooking liquid from **CROCK-POT**® slow cooker into sour cream mixture. Add mixture to **CROCK-POT**® slow cooker; mix well. Cook, uncovered, on HIGH 30 minutes or until thickened and bubbly. Serve over noodles.

Makes 8 servings

USE YOUR NOODLE

Simplify cooking tasty weeknight dinners
with these recipes for cooking noodle- or rice-filled
dishes right in your slow cooker

southwestern macaroni and cheese

    1   package (8 ounces) elbow macaroni
    1   can (14½ ounces) diced tomatoes with green pepper and onion,
        undrained
    1   can (10 ounces) diced tomatoes with green chilies, undrained
  1½   cups mild salsa
    3   cups (about 12 ounces) shredded Mexican cheese blend, divided

1. Lightly spray **CROCK-POT**® slow cooker with nonstick cooking spray. Stir
together macaroni, tomatoes with juice, salsa and 2 cups cheese in prepared
CROCK-POT® slow cooker. Cover and cook on LOW 3 hours and 45 minutes or
until macaroni is tender.

2. Sprinkle remaining 1 cup cheese over contents of **CROCK-POT**® slow cooker.
Cover and cook 15 minutes more or until cheese on top melts.

Makes 6 servings

cuban black beans and rice

. . . .

3¾ cups chicken broth

1½ cups uncooked brown rice

  1 large onion, chopped

  1 jalapeño pepper, seeded and chopped*

  3 cloves garlic, minced

  2 teaspoons ground cumin

  1 teaspoon salt

  2 cans (15 ounces each) black beans, rinsed and drained

  1 tablespoon fresh lime juice

    Sour cream (optional)

    Chopped green onions (optional)

. . . .

*Jalapeño peppers can sting and irritate the skin, so wear rubber gloves when handling peppers and do not touch eyes.

1. Place chicken broth, rice, onion, jalapeño, garlic, cumin and salt in **CROCK-POT®** slow cooker, mixing well. Cover and cook on LOW 7½ hours or until rice is tender.

2. Stir in beans and lime juice. Cover and cook 15 to 20 minutes more or until beans are heated through. Garnish with sour cream and green onions, if desired.

Makes 4 to 6 servings

greek rice

- 2 tablespoons butter
- 1¾ cups uncooked converted long-grain rice
- 2 cans (14 ounces each) low-sodium, fat-free chicken broth
- 1 teaspoon Greek seasoning
- 1 teaspoon ground oregano
- 1 cup pitted kalamata olives, drained and chopped
- ¾ cup chopped roasted red peppers
- Crumbled feta (optional)
- Fresh Italian parsley (optional)

1. Melt butter in large nonstick skillet over medium-high heat. Add rice and sauté 4 minutes or until golden brown. Transfer to **CROCK-POT®** slow cooker. Stir in chicken broth, Greek seasoning and oregano.

2. Cover and cook on LOW 4 hours or until liquid has all been absorbed and rice is tender. Stir in olives and roasted peppers and cook 5 minutes more. Garnish with feta and parsley, if desired.

Makes 6 to 8 servings

enffamilysoccerhomeworkmomdinnerballetchoresda
eakfast lessonsshoppingstudy
otherworkfootballscrapbookingminivanscheduleda

ziti ratatouille

· ·

- 1 large eggplant, peeled and cut into ½-inch cubes (about 1½ pounds)
- 2 medium zucchini, cut into ½-inch cubes
- 1 green or red bell pepper, seeded and cut into ½-inch pieces
- 1 large onion, chopped
- 4 cloves garlic, minced
- 1 jar (24 ounces) marinara sauce
- 2 cans (14½ ounces each) diced tomatoes with garlic and onion, undrained
- 1 can (6 ounces) pitted black olives, drained
- 1 package (8 ounces) ziti noodles
  Lemon juice (optional)
  Parmesan cheese (optional)

· ·

1. Combine eggplant, zucchini, bell pepper, onion, garlic, marinara sauce, tomatoes with juice and black olives in **CROCK-POT®** slow cooker. Cover and cook on LOW 4½ hours.

2. Stir in olives and pasta and cook 25 minutes more. Drizzle with fresh lemon juice and sprinkle with Parmesan cheese, if desired.

Makes 6 to 8 servings

thai chicken and noodles

- 2 teaspoons olive oil
- 1½ pounds boneless, skinless chicken breasts, sliced into thin strips
- 1 bottle (about 10 ounces) sweet chili sauce
- 3 tablespoons creamy peanut butter
- 3 cloves garlic, minced
- 1 can (14 ounces) chicken broth
- 1 package (8 ounces) vermicelli noodles
- 1 cup shredded cabbage and carrot mix
- 1 cup bean sprouts (optional)

  Chopped fresh cilantro (optional)

  Chopped roasted peanuts (optional)

1. Heat oil in large nonstick skillet over medium-high heat. Add chicken (in batches, if necessary) and cook, stirring frequently, until lightly browned on all sides. Transfer to **CROCK-POT®** slow cooker.

2. Stir together chili sauce, peanut butter and garlic in a small bowl. Pour over chicken. Stir until chicken is well coated with sauce. Add chicken broth and stir well. Cover and cook on LOW 2 hours.

3. Add noodles and cabbage mix. Cover and cook 30 more minutes or until noodles and cabbage are tender. Garnish with bean sprouts, chopped cilantro and peanuts, if desired.

Makes 4 to 6 servings

hoppin' john

- 1 package (16 ounces) andouille or smoked sausage, sliced
- 2½ cups chicken broth, divided
- 2 cans (15 ounces each) black-eyed peas, rinsed and drained
- 1 box (8 ounces) dirty rice mix
- ½ cup mild salsa
- ½ to ¾ cup lump crabmeat (optional)

1. Cook sausage in large skillet over medium heat, stirring frequently, 5 minutes or until browned all over; drain. Transfer to **CROCK-POT®** slow cooker. Return skillet to heat and pour in ½ cup chicken broth. Cook and stir scraping up any browned bits from skillet; pour over sausage.

2. Stir black-eyed peas, rice mix, remaining chicken broth and salsa into **CROCK-POT®** slow cooker with sausage. Cover and cook on LOW 3 to 4 hours or until rice is tender. Add crabmeat, if desired, and stir until well combined. Cover and cook until heated through, about 5 minutes.

Makes 6 servings

creamy chicken sausage rice pilaf

- 1 box (4 ounces) wild rice
- ½ cup brown basmati rice
- 1 package (12 ounces) fully cooked chicken apple sausage, cut into ½-inch slices
- 3 carrots, chopped
- 1 onion, chopped
- ½ cup dried cranberries
- 1 teaspoon dried oregano
- ¾ teaspoon salt
- ¼ teaspoon black pepper
- 3 cups water
- ½ cup heavy cream or half-and-half

Combine all ingredients except cream in **CROCK-POT**® slow cooker. Cover and cook on LOW 7 to 8 hours or until rice is tender. Turn off heat. Stir in cream and let stand 10 minutes before serving.

Makes 8 to 10 servings

italian sausage soup

Sausage Meatballs

- 1 pound mild Italian sausage, casings removed
- ½ cup dried bread crumbs
- ¼ cup grated Parmesan cheese
- ¼ cup milk
- 1 egg
- ½ teaspoon dried basil
- ½ teaspoon black pepper
- ¼ teaspoon garlic salt

Soup

- 4 cups hot chicken broth
- 1 tablespoon tomato paste
- 1 clove garlic, minced
- ¼ teaspoon red pepper flakes
- ½ cup uncooked mini pasta shells*
- 1 bag (10 ounces) baby spinach leaves
  Grated Parmesan cheese

*Or use other tiny pasta, such as ditalini (mini tubes) or farfallini (mini bow ties).

1. Combine all meatball ingredients. Form into marble-size balls.

2. Combine broth, tomato paste, garlic and red pepper flakes in **CROCK-POT®** slow cooker. Add meatballs. Cover; cook on LOW 5 to 6 hours.

3. Thirty minutes before serving, add pasta. When pasta is tender, stir in spinach leaves. Ladle into bowls, sprinkle with Parmesan cheese and serve immediately.

Makes 4 to 6 servings

penne pasta zuppa

- 1 can (15 ounces) white beans
- 2 medium yellow squash, diced
- 2 ripe tomatoes, diced
- 2 small red potatoes, cubed
- 2 leeks, sliced lengthwise into quarters then chopped
- 1 carrot, peeled and diced
- ¼ pound fresh green beans, washed, stemmed and diced
- 2 fresh sage leaves, minced
- 1 teaspoon salt
- ½ teaspoon black pepper
- 8 cups water
- ¼ pound uncooked penne pasta
- Grated Romano cheese (optional)

1. Combine beans, squash, tomatoes, potatoes, leeks, carrot, green beans, sage, salt and pepper in **CROCK-POT**® slow cooker. Add water. Stir well to combine. Cover; cook on HIGH 2 hours, stirring occasionally. Turn **CROCK-POT**® slow cooker to LOW. Cook, covered, 8 hours longer. Stir occasionally.

2. Turn **CROCK-POT**® slow cooker to HIGH. Add pasta. Cover; cook 30 minutes longer or until pasta is done.

3. To serve, garnish with Romano cheese, if desired.

Makes 6 servings

entfamilysoccerhomeworkmomdinnerballetchoresda
breakfast...lessonsshoppingstudy
motherworkfootballscrapbookingminivanscheduleda

rich and hearty drumstick soup

- 2 turkey drumsticks (about 1¾ pounds total)
- 3 carrots, peeled and sliced
- 3 stalks celery, thinly sliced
- 1 onion, chopped
- 2 cloves garlic, minced
- 1 teaspoon poultry seasoning
- 4 cups reduced-sodium chicken broth
- 3 cups water
- 8 ounces uncooked egg noodles
- ⅓ cup chopped parsley
- Salt and black pepper

1. Place drumsticks, carrots, celery, onion, garlic and poultry seasoning to **CROCK-POT®** slow cooker; pour in broth and water. Cover; cook on HIGH 5 hours or until meat is falling off bones.

2. Remove turkey; set aside. Add noodles; cover and cook 30 minutes more or until noodles are tender. Meanwhile, remove and discard skin and bones from turkey; shred meat.

3. Return turkey to **CROCK-POT®** slow cooker. Cover and cook until turkey is warmed through. Stir in parsley. Season to taste with salt and pepper.

Makes 8 servings

creamy farmhouse chicken and garden soup

- ½ package (16 ounces) frozen pepper stir-fry vegetable mix
- 1 cup frozen corn
- 1 medium zucchini, sliced
- 2 bone-in chicken thighs, skinned
- ½ teaspoon minced garlic
- 1 can (14 ounces) fat-free chicken broth
- ½ teaspoon dried thyme
- 2 ounces uncooked egg noodles
- 1 cup half-and-half
- ½ cup frozen green peas, thawed
- 2 tablespoons chopped parsley
- 2 tablespoons butter
- 1 teaspoon salt
- ½ teaspoon coarsely ground black pepper

note

To skin chicken easily, grasp skin with paper towel and pull away. Repeat with fresh paper towel for each piece of chicken, discarding skins and towels.

1. Coat **CROCK-POT®** slow cooker with nonstick cooking spray. Place stir-fry vegetables, corn and zucchini in bottom. Add chicken, garlic, broth and thyme. Cover; cook on HIGH 3 to 4 hours or until chicken is no longer pink in center. Remove chicken and set aside to cool slightly.

2. Add noodles to **CROCK-POT®** slow cooker. Cover; cook 20 minutes longer or until noodles are done.

3. Meanwhile, debone and chop chicken. Return to **CROCK-POT®** slow cooker. Stir in remaining ingredients. Let stand 5 minutes before serving.

Makes 4 servings

hearty chicken noodle soup

- 1¼ pounds boneless, skinless chicken breasts
- 1¼ pounds boneless, skinless chicken thighs
- 12 baby carrots, cut into ½-inch pieces
- 4 stalks celery, cut into ½-inch pieces
- ¾ cup finely chopped onion
- 1 teaspoon dried parsley flakes
- ½ teaspoon black pepper
- ¼ teaspoon cayenne pepper
- 1 teaspoon salt
- 4 cans (14½ ounces each) chicken broth
- 4 chicken-flavored bouillon cubes
- 2 cups uncooked egg noodles

1. Cut chicken into bite-size pieces. Place in **CROCK-POT®** slow cooker. Add carrots, celery, onion, parsley, black pepper, cayenne pepper, salt, chicken broth and bouillon cubes. Cover; cook on LOW 5 to 6 hours.

2. Stir in egg noodles. Turn temperature to HIGH. Cook 30 minutes longer or until noodles are tender.

Makes 8 to 10 servings

USE YOUR NOODLE

enfïamilysoccerhomeworkmomdinnerballetchoresda
breakfastessonsshoppingstudyi
prmotherworkfootballscrapbookingminivanscheduleda

creamy chicken and spinach lasagna

1¼ cups shredded Swiss or mozzarella cheese, divided

  1 cup ricotta cheese

  1 teaspoon dried oregano

 ¼ teaspoon red pepper flakes

  1 container (10 ounces) refrigerated Alfredo pasta sauce

 ⅓ cup water

  4 no-boil lasagna noodles

  1 package (10 ounces) frozen chopped spinach, thawed and squeezed dry

1½ cups cooked diced chicken

 ¼ cup grated Parmesan cheese

    Red pepper flakes (optional)

1. Combine 1 cup Swiss cheese, ricotta, oregano and pepper flakes in small bowl; set aside. Blend Alfredo sauce with water; set aside.

2. Coat **CROCK-POT**® slow cooker with nonstick cooking spray. Break 2 lasagna noodles in half and place on bottom. Spread half of ricotta mixture over noodles. Top with half of spinach. Arrange half of chicken and half of Parmesan over spinach. Pour half of Alfredo mixture over top. Repeat layers, beginning with noodles and ending with Alfredo mixture. Cover; cook on LOW 3 hours.

3. Sprinkle remaining ¼ cup Swiss cheese on top. Cover and let stand 5 minutes or until cheese is melted. To serve, cut into squares or wedges. Garnish with pepper flakes, if desired.

Makes 4 servings

mediterranean tomato, oregano and orzo soup

- 2 tablespoons extra-virgin olive oil
- 1 large yellow onion, cut into wedges
- 3½ cups fresh tomatoes, peeled* and crushed
- 2 cups butternut squash, peeled and cut into ½-inch cubes
- 1 cup carrots, peeled and cut into matchstick pieces
- ½ cup zucchini, cleaned and sliced
- 1 tablespoon minced fresh bay leaves or 3 whole dried bay leaves
- 1 tablespoon chopped fresh oregano
- 1 can (15 ounces) garbanzo beans, drained and rinsed
- 2 cups chicken broth
- 1 clove garlic, minced
- 1 teaspoon ground cumin
- ¾ teaspoon ground allspice
- ½ teaspoon salt
- ¼ teaspoon black pepper
- 1½ cups uncooked orzo pasta

*To peel tomatoes, place one at a time in simmering water about 10 seconds. (Add 30 seconds if tomatoes are not fully ripened.) Immediately plunge into a bowl of cold water for another 10 seconds. Peel skin with a knife.

1. Heat oil in skillet over medium heat until hot. Add onion. Cook and stir until translucent and soft, about 10 minutes.

2. Add tomatoes, squash, carrots, zucchini, bay leaves and oregano to skillet. Cook and stir 25 to 30 minutes longer. Transfer to **CROCK-POT®** slow cooker.

3. Add remaining ingredients except orzo pasta. Cover; cook on LOW 7 to 8 hours or on HIGH 4 to 5 hours.

4. Turn **CROCK-POT®** slow cooker to HIGH. Add orzo. Cover; cook 30 to 45 minutes or until pasta is done. (Remove dried bay leaves before serving, if used.)

Makes 6 servings

pasta fagioli soup

- 2 cans (about 14 ounces each) reduced-sodium beef or vegetable broth
- 1 can (about 15 ounces) Great Northern beans, rinsed and drained
- 1 can (about 14 ounces) diced tomatoes, drained
- 2 medium zucchini, quartered lengthwise and sliced
- 1 tablespoon olive oil
- 1½ teaspoons minced garlic
- ½ teaspoon dried basil
- ½ teaspoon dried oregano
- ½ cup uncooked tubetti, ditalini or small shell pasta
- ½ cup garlic seasoned croutons
- ½ cup grated Asiago or Romano cheese
- 3 tablespoons chopped fresh basil or Italian parsley (optional)

1. Combine broth, beans, tomatoes, zucchini, oil, garlic, basil and oregano in **CROCK-POT**® slow cooker; mix well. Cover; cook on LOW 3 to 4 hours.

2. Stir in pasta. Cover; cook on LOW 1 hour or until pasta is tender.

3. Serve soup with croutons and cheese. Garnish with fresh basil, if desired.

Makes 5 to 6 servings

tip

Only use small pasta varieties like tubetti, ditalini or small shell-shaped pasta in this recipe. The low heat of a slow cooker won't allow larger pasta shapes to cook completely.

no-fuss macaroni & cheese

- 2 cups (about 8 ounces) uncooked elbow macaroni
- 4 ounces light pasteurized processed cheese, cubed
- 1 cup (4 ounces) shredded mild Cheddar cheese
- ½ teaspoon salt
- ⅛ teaspoon black pepper
- 1½ cups fat-free (skim) milk

Combine macaroni, cheeses, salt and pepper in **CROCK-POT**® slow cooker. Pour milk over all. Cover; cook on LOW 2 to 3 hours, stirring after 20 to 30 minutes.

Makes 6 to 8 servings

THE COMPLETE PACKAGE

Convenient pre-prepped ingredients such as bagged frozen vegetables and rice or pasta mixes make these recipes a snap to prepare

carne rellenos

1 can (4 ounces) whole green chilies, drained
4 ounces cream cheese, softened
1 flank steak (about 2 pounds)
1½ cups prepared salsa verde

1. Slit whole chilies open on 1 side with sharp knife; stuff with cream cheese.

2. Open steak flat on sheet of waxed paper; score steak and turn over. Lay stuffed chilies across unscored side of steak. Roll up and tie with kitchen string.

3. Place steak in the **CROCK-POT**® slow cooker; pour in salsa. Cover; cook on LOW 6 to 8 hours or on HIGH 3 to 4 hours or until done.

4. Remove steak and cut into 6 pieces. Serve with sauce.

Makes 6 servings

beef and black bean chili

- 1 tablespoon vegetable oil
- 1 pound beef stew meat
- 1 can (14 ounces) green and red pepper strips with onions
- 1 can (15 ounces) black beans, drained and rinsed
- 1 can (14½ ounces) fired-roasted diced tomatoes, undrained
- 2 tablespoons chili powder
- 1 tablespoon minced garlic
- 2 teaspoons ground cumin
- ½ ounce semi-sweet chocolate, chopped
- 2 cups hot cooked white rice
  Shredded Cheddar cheese (optional)
  Sour cream (optional)

1. Heat oil in large skillet over medium-high heat. Add beef and cook, turning occasionally, until browned on all sides, about 5 minutes. Transfer to **CROCK-POT**® slow cooker.

2. Stir in pepper strips, beans, tomatoes with juice, chili powder, garlic and cumin. Cover and cook on LOW 8 to 9 hours.

3. Turn off heat and stir in chocolate until melted. Serve over rice. Garnish with Cheddar cheese and sour cream, if desired.

Makes 4 servings

shepherd's pie

- 1 pound lean ground beef
- 1 pound ground lamb
- 1 package (12 ounces) frozen chopped onion
- 2 tablespoons minced garlic
- 1 can (about 14 ounces) diced tomatoes, drained
- 1 package (12 ounces) frozen peas and carrots
- 3 tablespoons quick-cooking tapioca
- 2 teaspoons dried oregano
- 1 teaspoon salt
- ½ teaspoon black pepper
- 2 packages (24 ounces each) prepared mashed potatoes

1. Cook beef and lamb in large nonstick skillet over medium-high heat, stirring occasionally, until no longer pink. Transfer to **CROCK-POT®** slow cooker. Return skillet to heat and add onion and garlic. Cook, stirring frequently, until onions begin to soften, about 4 to 5 minutes. Transfer to **CROCK-POT®** slow cooker with beef and lamb.

2. Stir in tomatoes, peas and carrots, tapioca, oregano, salt and pepper. Cover and cook on LOW 7 to 8 hours. Top with prepared mashed potatoes. Cover and cook on LOW until potatoes are heated through, about 30 minutes.

Makes 6 servings

leek and potato soup

- 6 slices bacon, chopped
- 1 package (32 ounces) frozen shredded hash brown potatoes
- 3 leeks, white and light green parts only, cut into ¾-inch pieces
- 1 can (10¾ ounces) condensed cream of potato soup, undiluted
- 1 can (14½ ounces) reduced-sodium chicken broth
- 2 ribs celery, sliced
- 1 can (5 ounces) evaporated milk
- ½ cup sour cream

1. Cook bacon in large skillet over medium-high heat, stirring occasionally, until crisp and browned, about 5 to 6 minutes. Remove with a slotted spoon and drain on paper towel-lined plate.

2. Combine bacon, potatoes, leeks, soup, broth, celery and evaporated milk in **CROCK-POT**® slow cooker. Cover and cook on LOW 6 to 7 hours. Stir in sour cream and serve.

Makes 4 to 6 servings

cinnamon roll-topped mixed berry cobbler

- 2 **bags (12 ounces each) frozen mixed berries**
- 1 **cup sugar**
- ¼ **cup quick-cooking tapioca**
- ¼ **cup water**
- 2 **teaspoons vanilla**
- 1 **package (about 12 ounces) refrigerated cinnamon rolls with icing**

Stir together berries, sugar, tapioca, water and vanilla in 4-quart **CROCK-POT®** slow cooker. Top with cinnamon rolls. Cover and cook on LOW 4 to 5 hours. Spread or drizzle icing on tops of rolls just before serving.

Makes 8 servings

thai coconut chicken and rice soup

- 1 pound boneless, skinless chicken thighs, cut into 1-inch pieces
- 3 cups reduced-sodium chicken broth
- 1½ cups frozen chopped onions
- 1 can (4 ounces) sliced mushrooms, drained
- 2 tablespoons minced fresh ginger
- 2 tablespoons sugar
- 1 cup cooked rice
- 1 can (15 ounces) unsweetened coconut milk
- ½ red bell pepper, seeded and thinly sliced
- 3 tablespoons chopped fresh cilantro
- 2 teaspoons grated fresh lime zest

1. Combine chicken, broth, onions, mushrooms, ginger and sugar in **CROCK-POT®** slow cooker. Cover and cook on LOW 8 to 9 hours.

2. Stir rice, coconut milk and bell pepper into soup. Cover and cook 15 minutes longer. Turn off heat and stir in cilantro and lime zest.

Makes 6 to 8 servings

barbecued pulled pork sandwiches

1 pork shoulder roast (about 2½ pounds)

1 bottle (14 ounces) barbecue sauce

1 tablespoon fresh lemon juice

1 teaspoon brown sugar

1 medium onion, chopped

8 hamburger buns or hard rolls

1. Place pork roast in **CROCK-POT®** slow cooker. Cover; cook on LOW 10 to 12 hours or on HIGH 5 to 6 hours.

2. Remove pork roast from **CROCK-POT®** slow cooker. Shred with 2 forks. Discard cooking liquid. Return pork to **CROCK-POT®** slow cooker; add barbecue sauce, lemon juice, brown sugar and onion. Cover and cook on LOW 2 hours or on HIGH 1 hour. Serve pork on hamburger buns or hard rolls.

Makes 8 servings

note

This kid-popular dish is sweet and savory, and most importantly, extremely easy to make. Serve with crunchy coleslaw on the side.

tip

For a 5-, 6- or 7-quart **CROCK-POT®** slow cooker, double all ingredients except for the barbecue sauce. Increase the barbecue sauce to 21 ounces.

chicken & biscuits

- 4 boneless, skinless chicken breasts
- 1 can (10¾ ounces) condensed cream of chicken soup
- 1 package (10 ounces) frozen peas and carrots
- 1 package (7½ ounces) refrigerated biscuits

1. Cut chicken breasts into bite-size pieces. Place in **CROCK-POT®** slow cooker. Pour soup over chicken. Cover; cook on LOW 4 hours or until chicken is tender and no longer pink in center.

2. Stir in frozen vegetables. Cover and cook 30 minutes longer until vegetables are heated through.

3. Bake biscuits according to package directions. Spoon chicken and vegetable mixture over biscuits and serve.

Makes 4 servings

cream cheese chicken with broccoli

- 4 pounds boneless, skinless chicken breasts, cut into ½-inch pieces
- 1 tablespoon olive oil
- 1 package (1 ounce) Italian salad dressing mix
- 1 package (8 ounces) sliced fresh mushrooms
- 1 cup chopped onion
- 1 can (10¾ ounces) condensed low-fat cream of chicken soup, undiluted
- 1 bag (10 ounces) frozen broccoli florets, thawed
- 1 package (8 ounces) low-fat cream cheese, cubed
- ¼ cup dry sherry
  Hot cooked pasta

1. Toss chicken with olive oil. Sprinkle with Italian salad dressing mix. Place in **CROCK-POT**® slow cooker. Cover; cook on LOW 3 hours.

2. Coat large skillet with nonstick cooking spray. Add mushrooms and onion; cook 5 minutes over medium heat or until onion is tender, stirring occasionally.

3. Add soup, broccoli, cream cheese and sherry to skillet; cook and stir until hot. Transfer to **CROCK-POT**® slow cooker. Cover; cook on LOW 1 hour. Serve chicken and sauce over pasta.

Makes 10 to 12 servings

tip

For easier preparation, cut up the chicken and vegetables for this recipe the night before. Don't place the **CROCK-POT**® stoneware in the refrigerator. Instead, wrap the chicken and vegetables separately, and store in the refrigerator.

vegetable curry

- 4 baking potatoes, diced
- 1 large onion, chopped
- 1 red bell pepper, chopped
- 2 carrots, diced
- 2 tomatoes, chopped
- 1 can (6 ounces) tomato paste
- ¾ cup water
- 2 teaspoons cumin seeds
- ½ teaspoon garlic powder
- ½ teaspoon salt
- ½ package (about 3 cups) frozen cauliflower florets
- 1 package (10 ounces) frozen peas, thawed

Combine potatoes, onion, bell pepper, carrots and tomatoes in **CROCK-POT**® slow cooker. Stir in tomato paste, water, cumin seeds, garlic powder and salt. Add cauliflower; stir well. Cover; cook on LOW 8 to 9 hours or until vegetables are tender. Stir in peas; cover and cook about 5 minutes to warm peas before serving.

Makes 6 servings

easy beef stew

- 2 pounds beef stew meat, cut into 1-inch cubes
- 1 can (4 ounces) mushrooms
- 1 envelope (1 ounce) dry onion soup mix
- ⅓ cup red or white wine
- 1 can (10 ounces) condensed cream of mushroom soup, undiluted
   Hot cooked noodles

Combine all ingredients except noodles in **CROCK-POT®** slow cooker. Cover; cook on LOW 8 to 12 hours. Serve over noodles.

Makes 4 to 6 servings

tip

Browning the beef before cooking it in the **CROCK-POT®** slow cooker isn't necessary but helps to enhance the flavor and appearance of the stew. If you have the time, use nonstick cooking spray and brown the meat in a large skillet before placing it in the **CROCK-POT®** slow cooker; follow the recipe as written.

southwest chipotle turkey sloppy joe hoagies

- 1 pound turkey Italian sausage, casings removed
- 1 bag (14 ounces) frozen green and red pepper strips with onions
- 1 can (6 ounces) tomato paste
- 1 tablespoon quick-cooking tapioca
- 1 tablespoon minced chipotle pepper in adobo sauce, plus 1 tablespoon sauce
- 2 teaspoons ground cumin
- ½ teaspoon dried thyme
- 4 hoagie rolls, split horizontally

1. Cook sausage in medium nonstick skillet over medium-high heat, stirring frequently to break up meat, until no longer pink. Transfer to **CROCK-POT®** slow cooker.

2. Stir in pepper strips, tomato paste, tapioca, chipotle and sauce, cumin and thyme. Cover and cook on LOW 8 to 10 hours. Serve in hoagie rolls.

Makes 4 servings

slow cooker chicken dinner

- 4 boneless, skinless chicken breasts
- 1 can (10¾ ounces) condensed cream of chicken soup, undiluted
- ⅓ cup milk
- 1 package (6 ounces) stuffing mix
- 1⅔ cups water

1. Place chicken in **CROCK-POT®** slow cooker. Combine soup and milk in small bowl; mix well. Pour soup mixture over chicken.

2. Combine stuffing mix and water. Spoon stuffing over chicken. Cover; cook on LOW 6 to 8 hours.

Makes 4 servings

sweet and sour shrimp with pineapple

- 3 cans (8 ounces each) pineapple chunks, drained, plus 1 cup juice reserved
- 2 packages (6 ounces each) frozen snow peas, thawed
- ¼ cup cornstarch
- ⅓ cup sugar, plus 2 teaspoons
- 2 chicken bouillon cubes
- 2 cups boiling water
- 4 teaspoons soy sauce
- 1 teaspoon ground ginger
- 1 pound frozen peeled, deveined shrimp, unthawed
- ¼ cup cider vinegar

  Hot cooked rice

1. Drain pineapple chunks, reserving 1 cup juice. Place pineapple and snow peas in **CROCK-POT®** slow cooker.

2. Combine cornstarch and sugar in medium saucepan. Dissolve bouillon cubes in water and add to saucepan. Mix in 1 cup reserved pineapple juice, soy sauce and ginger. Bring to a boil and cook 1 minute. Pour into **CROCK-POT®** slow cooker. Cover; cook on LOW 4½ to 5½ hours.

3. Add shrimp and vinegar. Cover; cook on LOW 30 minutes or until shrimp are done. Serve over hot rice.

Makes 4 servings

shredded beef fajitas

- 1 beef flank steak (about 1½ pounds)
- 1 can (14½ ounces) diced tomatoes with jalapeños, undrained*
- 1 cup chopped onion
- 1 medium green bell pepper, cut into ½-inch pieces
- 2 cloves garlic, minced or ¼ teaspoon garlic powder
- 1 package (about 1½ ounces) fajita seasoning mix
- 12 (8-inch) flour tortillas

Optional toppings: reduced-fat sour cream, guacamole, shredded reduced-fat Cheddar cheese, salsa

*Jalapeño peppers can sting and irritate the skin, so wear rubber gloves when handling peppers and do not touch eyes.

1. Cut flank steak into 6 portions; place in **CROCK-POT®** slow cooker. Combine tomatoes with juice, onion, bell pepper, garlic and fajita seasoning mix in medium bowl. Pour over steak. Cover; cook on LOW 8 to 10 hours, on HIGH 4 to 5 hours or until beef is tender.

2. Remove beef from **CROCK-POT®** slow cooker; shred with 2 forks. Return beef to **CROCK-POT®** slow cooker and stir.

3. To serve fajitas, place meat mixture evenly into flour tortillas. Add toppings as desired; roll up tortillas.

Makes 12 servings

easy beef stroganoff

- 3 cans (10¾ ounces each) condensed cream of mushroom soup, undiluted
- 1 cup sour cream
- ½ cup water
- 1 package (1 ounce) dry onion soup mix
- 2 pounds beef stew meat, cut into 1-inch pieces

Combine soup, sour cream, water and soup mix in **CROCK-POT**® slow cooker. Add beef; stir until well coated. Cover; cook on LOW 6 hours or on HIGH 3 hours.

Makes 4 to 6 servings

DOUBLE DUTY

Cooking tonight gives you a head start on dinner
tomorrow with these matched recipes where planned
leftovers from one meal are the base for another

autumn herbed chicken with fennel and squash

3 to 4 pounds chicken thighs
  Salt and black pepper, to taste
  All-purpose flour, as needed
2 tablespoons olive oil
1 fennel bulb, thinly sliced
½ butternut squash, peeled, seeded and cut into ¾-inch cubes
1 teaspoon dried thyme
¾ cup walnuts (optional)
¾ cup chicken broth
½ cup apple cider or juice
  Cooked rice or pasta
¼ cup fresh basil, sliced into ribbons
2 teaspoons fresh rosemary, finely minced

1. Season chicken on all sides with salt and pepper, then lightly coat with flour. Heat oil in skillet over medium heat until hot. Brown chicken in batches to prevent crowding. Brown on each side 3 to 5 minutes, turning once. Remove with slotted spoon. Transfer to **CROCK-POT®** slow cooker.

2. Add fennel, squash and thyme. Stir well to combine. Add walnuts, if desired, broth and cider. Cover; cook on LOW 5 to 7 hours or on HIGH 2½ to 4½ hours.

3. If desired, reserve ⅓ of chicken (about 1 pound total) for Chicken Pot Pie (see page 78). Serve remaining chicken and vegetables over rice or pasta, and garnish with basil and fresh rosemary.

Makes 4 servings

chicken pot pie

- 1 pound cooked chicken (reserved from Autumn Herbed Chicken with Fennel and Squash, see page 76)
- 3 tablespoons butter
- 1 medium onion, chopped
- 1 cup sliced celery
- ⅓ cup all-purpose flour
- 1½ cups reduced-fat (2%) milk
- 1 cup chicken broth
- 2 cups frozen mixed vegetables (broccoli, carrots and cauliflower combination), thawed
- 1 tablespoon chopped fresh parsley or 1 teaspoon dried parsley
- ½ teaspoon dried thyme leaves
- 1 (9-inch) refrigerated pie crust
- 1 egg, lightly beaten

1. Remove any skin and bones from cooked chicken and discard. Cut chicken into ½-inch pieces and set aside.

2. Melt butter in medium saucepan over medium heat. Add onion and celery. Cook and stir 3 minutes. Stir in flour until well blended. Gradually stir in milk and broth. Cook, stirring constantly, until sauce thickens and boils. Add chicken, vegetables, parsley and thyme. Pour into 1½-quart deep casserole.

3. Preheat oven to 400°F. Roll out pie crust 1 inch larger than diameter of casserole on lightly floured surface. Cut slits in crust to vent; place on top of casserole. Roll edges and cut away extra dough; flute edges. If desired, reroll scraps to cut into decorative designs; place on crust. Brush pastry with beaten egg. Bake about 30 minutes or until crust is golden brown and filling is bubbly.

Makes 4 to 6 servings

tip

2 cups diced cooked chicken, 1 can (14½ ounces) chicken broth, ¼ teaspoon salt and ¼ teaspoon black pepper can be substituted for the first 4 ingredients.

nffamilysoccerhomeworkmomdinnerballetchoresdad
reakfast lessonsshoppingstudyingtr
rotherworkfootballscrapbookingminivanscheduled

DOUBLE DUTY

braised turkey breasts
with lemon-artichoke heart sauce

- 2 bone-in, skin on turkey breast halves (about 2 pounds each)
- 2 teaspoons salt, plus additional for seasoning
- ¼ teaspoon pepper, plus additional for seasoning
- ½ cup all-purpose flour
- 4 teaspoons vegetable oil, divided
- 4 large shallots, peeled and thinly sliced (about 1 cup total)
- ½ cup dry sherry
- 1 lemon, cut into ¼-inch-thick slices
- 2 tablespoons capers, rinsed and drained
- 4 thyme sprigs
- 1½ cups low-sodium chicken broth
- 2 cans (about 14 ounces each) artichoke hearts, drained
- 2 tablespoons finely chopped flat-leaf parsley
  Hot cooked egg noodles (optional)

1. Season both sides of turkey breasts liberally with salt and pepper. Dredge in flour, shaking off excess. Warm 2 teaspoons oil in large skillet over medium-high heat. Add 1 turkey breast half, and cook until brown on both sides, about 4 minutes total. Transfer to **CROCK-POT®** slow cooker. Repeat with remaining 2 teaspoons oil and second turkey breast; transfer to **CROCK-POT®** slow cooker.

2. Reduce heat to medium and add shallots to skillet. Cook until softened and just beginning to brown, about 4 minutes. Add sherry and stir to scrape up browned bits from bottom of pan. Cook until pan is almost dry, about 30 seconds, then pour over turkey breasts. Add lemon slices, capers, thyme sprigs, 2 teaspoons salt and ¼ teaspoon pepper. Pour in chicken broth. Cover and cook on LOW 6 hours or until turkey breasts are tender and nearly falling off the bone.

3. Remove turkey breasts; set aside to cool 10 minutes. Remove and discard skin and bones.

4. Meanwhile, remove thyme from cooking liquid; discard. Skim fat from sauce. Stir in artichoke hearts and chopped parsley. Season to taste with salt and pepper. Slice turkey and serve over noodles topped with Lemon-Artichoke Heart Sauce. If desired, reserve ½ cup strained artichoke sauce mixture and 1 cup sliced turkey for Turkey-Artichoke Spanish Tortilla (see page 82) before serving.

Makes 6 servings

turkey-artichoke spanish tortilla

- 10 eggs
- 1 cup sliced turkey breast (reserved from Braised Turkey Breasts with Lemon-Artichoke Heart Sauce, see page 80), finely chopped
- ½ cup Artichoke-Lemon Sauce (reserved from Braised Turkey Breasts with Lemon-Artichoke Heart Sauce, see page 80)
- 1¼ cups shredded Pecorino Romano cheese (about 4½ ounces)
- 1½ teaspoons salt
- ½ teaspoon ground black pepper
- ¼ cup plus 2 tablespoons olive oil, divided
- 1 package (20 ounces) refrigerated ready-to-cook shredded hash brown potatoes
- 1 cup diced onion
- 4 cloves garlic, minced

1. Set oven rack to upper-middle position and preheat oven to 400°F.

2. Beat eggs in large bowl. Stir in chopped turkey, Lemon-Artichoke Heart Sauce, cheese, salt and pepper. Set aside.

3. Heat 2 tablespoons oil in 12-inch oven-safe nonstick skillet over medium-high heat. Add hash browns and onion and cook until both are tender, about 12 minutes, stirring occasionally. Add garlic and cook 1 minute, stirring constantly. Reduce heat to medium.

4. Stir potatoes and onions into egg mixture. Return pan to heat and warm remaining ¼ cup oil. Pour potato and egg mixture into prepared skillet, pressing into pan to form solid cake. Cook until edges of eggs are set, 14 minutes, running thin spatula around side of pan occasionally to prevent sticking. Transfer skillet to oven and bake until puffed and almost entirely set, 12 minutes.

5. Preheat broiler. Broil 2 minutes, until golden brown and eggs are completely set. Wearing oven mitt, remove skillet from oven; let stand 5 minutes. Carefully invert tortilla onto large plate or cutting board. Let stand 5 minutes to fully set. Cut into wedges and serve.

Makes 8 to 10 servings

beef pasties

¼ pound small red potatoes, cut into ¼-inch dice (about 1 cup)

1 large carrot, cut into ¼-inch dice (about 1 cup)

1 tablespoon water

4 cooked beef short ribs, bones removed and meat shredded (reserved from Bacon Onion Stout Short Ribs, see page 84)

½ cup sauce (reserved from Bacon, Onion & Stout Braised Short Ribs, see page 84)

¼ cup frozen peas, thawed

2 cans (about 16 ounces each) large refrigerated flaky biscuits

1 egg, beaten with 1 teaspoon water

1. Preheat oven to 350°F. Lightly coat two baking sheets with nonstick cooking spray.

2. Place potatoes, carrot and 1 tablespoon water in microwave-safe bowl and cover with plastic wrap. Microwave 2 minutes, or until tender. Drain liquid from bowl.

3. Combine shredded beef, reserved sauce, peas, cooked potatoes and carrot in medium bowl, making about 4 cups filling total.

4. Roll out 1 biscuit into a 5-inch round on a lightly floured surface. Mound scant ¼ cup filling on half of biscuit. Brush edge of biscuit with egg wash. Fold dough over beef and pinch edges closed. Crimp edges shut securely. Carefully transfer to prepared baking sheet. Repeat with remaining biscuits and beef mixture.

5. Brush tops of pasties with remaining egg wash. Pierce each pasty twice with fork to allow steam to escape while baking. Bake until golden brown, about 25 minutes, rotating pans from top to bottom and turning 180 degrees halfway through baking. Let cool 10 minutes before serving.

Makes 8 servings (2 pasties per serving)

bacon, onion & stout braised short ribs

- 4 pounds bone-in beef short ribs, visible fat trimmed
- 1 teaspoon salt, plus additional for seasoning
- ½ teaspoon ground black pepper, plus additional for seasoning
- 1 tablespoon vegetable oil
- 6 ounces thick-cut bacon, cut into ¼-inch dice
- 1 large onion, halved and cut into ¼-inch-thick slices
- 1 tablespoon minced garlic
- 1 tablespoon tomato paste
- 2 tablespoons all-purpose flour
- 2 tablespoons spicy brown mustard
- 1 bottle (12 ounces) Irish stout
- 1 bay leaf
- 1 cup beef broth
- 2 tablespoons finely chopped parsley leaves
- Hot mashed potatoes or cooked egg noodles (optional)

cook's tip

This recipe only gets better if made ahead and refrigerated overnight. This makes skimming any fat from the surface easier, too.

1. Season beef with salt and pepper. Heat oil in large skillet over medium-high heat until almost smoking. Working in batches, cook short ribs in skillet, turning to brown all sides. Transfer each batch to **CROCK-POT®** slow cooker as it is finished. Wipe out pan with paper towels and return to heat.

2. Cook bacon, stirring occasionally, until crisp, about 4 minutes. Transfer with slotted spoon to paper towel-lined plate to drain. Remove and discard all but 1 tablespoon drippings from pan. Reduce heat to medium and add onion. Cook until softened and translucent, stirring occasionally. Add garlic, tomato paste, flour, mustard, 1 teaspoon salt and ½ teaspoon pepper. Cook, stirring constantly, 1 minute. Remove skillet from heat and pour in stout, stirring to scrape browned bits from bottom of pan. Pour over short ribs. Add drained bacon, bay leaf and beef broth. Cover and cook on LOW 8 hours or until meat is tender and falls off the bone.

3. Remove beef and skim fat from cooking liquid. Remove bay leaf and stir in parsley. If desired, reserve 4 short ribs and ½ cup sauce for Beef Pasties (see page 83). Serve remaining short ribs with mashed potatoes or wide egg noodles.

Makes 4 to 6 servings

spicy sausage bolognese sauce

- 2 tablespoons olive oil, divided
- 1 pound ground beef
- 1 pound hot Italian sausage, casings removed
- ¼ pound pancetta, diced
- 1 large onion, finely diced (about 2¾ cups)
- 2 medium carrots, peeled and finely diced (about 1 cup)
- 1 large celery stalk, finely diced (about ¾ cups)
- ½ teaspoon salt
- ½ teaspoon ground black pepper
- 1 tablespoon minced garlic
- 3 tablespoons tomato paste
- 2 cans (28 ounces each) diced tomatoes, drained
- ¾ cup whole milk
- ¾ cup dry red wine
- 1 pound hot cooked spaghetti
- ½ cup grated Parmesan cheese (optional)

1. Heat 1 tablespoon olive oil in large skillet over medium-high heat. Add ground beef and Italian sausage. Cook until no longer pink, stirring to break up meat. Transfer to **CROCK-POT®** slow cooker with slotted spoon. Discard drippings and wipe out pan with paper towel; return to heat.

2. Add remaining 1 tablespoon olive oil. Add pancetta and cook until crisp and browned, stirring occasionally. Using a slotted spoon, transfer to **CROCK-POT®** slow cooker.

3. Reduce heat to medium and add onion, carrots, celery, salt and pepper. Cook, stirring occasionally, until onion is translucent and carrots and celery are just tender. Stir in garlic and tomato paste and cook 1 minute, stirring constantly. Transfer to **CROCK-POT®** slow cooker. Stir in tomatoes, milk and wine. Cover and cook on LOW 6 hours. Reserve 5 cups sauce for Spinach Bolognese Lasagna (see page 88) or another use. Toss remaining 6 cups sauce with hot cooked spaghetti and sprinkle with Parmesan cheese, if desired, just before serving.

Makes 6 to 10 servings

DOUBLE DUTY

spinach bolognese lasagna

- **2** teaspoons olive oil
- **1** tablespoon minced garlic
- **12** ounces baby spinach
- **1** container (15 ounces) ricotta cheese
- **½** cup finely chopped basil
- **½** cup grated Parmesan cheese
- **1** teaspoon salt
- **¼** teaspoon ground black pepper
- **1** box (9 ounces) no-boil lasagna noodles (16 noodles)
- **5** cups sauce (reserved from Spicy Sausage Bolognese Sauce, see page 86)*
- **10** ounces shredded mozzarella cheese (about 2½ cups)

Note: The meat in the refrigerated Bolognese sauce may absorb some of the sauce and reduce volume of sauce from 5 cups to about 3¾ cups. Allow sauce to come to room temperature in a large glass measure and stir in enough water to bring total to 5 cups before proceeding.

1. Preheat oven to 400°F. Coat 13 × 9-inch baking dish with nonstick cooking spray. Coat 18-inch piece of foil with cooking spray; set aside.

2. Heat olive oil in large skillet over medium heat. Add garlic and cook 1 minute, stirring occasionally. Add spinach and cook until just wilted, 3 to 4 minutes. Remove to sieve and cool slightly. Press out as much liquid as possible. Transfer to medium bowl and stir in ricotta, basil, Parmesan cheese, salt and pepper until well combined; set aside.

3. Place lasagna noodles in a large bowl and cover with hot water; soak 5 minutes. Remove noodles and set on clean kitchen towels; cover with additional towels to keep moist.

4. Spread ¾ cup Bolognese sauce in bottom of prepared baking dish. Arrange 4 noodles on sauce. Top with 1 cup ricotta mixture, another 1 cup Bolognese sauce and ½ cup mozzarella cheese. Repeat layers once. Repeat layers a second time but use remaining 1⅓ cups ricotta mixture and omit Bolognese sauce. Top with remaining 4 noodles, remaining Bolognese sauce and remaining mozzarella cheese. Cover with prepared foil. Bake until cheese is melted and bubbly and filling is hot, 30 to 45 minutes. Remove foil and broil until cheese is spotty brown, about 3 minutes. Let cool 10 minutes before slicing and serving.

Makes 10 to 12 servings (one 13 × 9-inch lasagna)

ntfamilysoccerhomeworkmomdinnerballetchoresda
akfast lessonsshoppingstudyingtrac
therworkfootballscrapbookingminivanscheduleda

DOUBLE DUTY

chicken biryani

- 3 tablespoons unsalted butter
- 1 medium onion, diced (about 1 cup)
- 2 jalapeño peppers, seeded and finely diced*
- 3 cloves garlic, minced
- 3 green cardamom pods**
- 2 cups long-grain white rice, such as basmati rice
- 2 cups water
- 1 teaspoon salt
- 1 cup curry (reserved from Indian-Style Curried Drumsticks, see page 90)
- ¼ cup raisins
- 4 chicken drumsticks (reserved from Indian-Style Curried Drumsticks see page 90), bones removed
- ¼ cup chopped fresh cilantro
- ¼ cup chopped fresh mint
- ⅓ cup coarsely chopped roasted unsalted cashews

*Jalapeño peppers can sting and irritate the skin, so wear rubber gloves when handling peppers and do not touch eyes.

**If whole green cardamom pods are unavailable, substitute scant ½ teaspoon ground cardamom.

1. Melt butter in 4-quart heavy-bottomed saucepan over medium heat. Add onion and cook, stirring frequently, until softened and golden, about 5 minutes. Add jalapeño peppers, garlic, cardamom and rice and cook, stirring constantly, until rice is toasted, 2 to 3 minutes.

2. Stir in water, salt, reserved curry, raisins and meat from reserved drumsticks. Bring to a boil. Reduce heat to low, cover and simmer until rice is tender and most of liquid has evaporated, 10 to 15 minutes. Using a rubber spatula, fluff rice and fold in cilantro, mint and cashews just before serving.

Makes 4 to 6 servings

indian-style curried drumsticks

- 12 chicken drumsticks, skin removed (about 3 pounds)
- 1 cinnamon stick
- 2 tablespoons vegetable oil
- 1 large onion, diced (about 2 cups total)
- 1 tablespoon grated ginger
- 1 tablespoon minced garlic
- 3 tablespoons tomato paste
- 1 teaspoon ground coriander
- 1 tablespoon ground cumin
- 2 teaspoons ground turmeric
- 2 teaspoons salt
- ½ teaspoon ground black pepper
- 8 medium red potatoes, cut in half
- 1¼ cups low-sodium chicken broth
- 1 cup frozen peas

cook's tip

To remove skin from drumsticks easily, use a paper towel to help grab onto the skin before pulling it off in the direction of the bone.

1. Place drumsticks and cinnamon stick in **CROCK-POT®** slow cooker.

2. Heat oil in medium saucepan over medium heat. Add onion and cook, stirring frequently, until softened, about 6 minutes. Add ginger, garlic, tomato paste, spices, salt and pepper and cook 2 minutes, stirring constantly. Transfer mixture to **CROCK-POT®** slow cooker.

3. Add potatoes and chicken broth. Cover and cook on LOW until chicken almost falls off the bone, 6 hours.

4. Remove potatoes and stir in peas. Cover and cook 5 minutes more to warm peas. If desired, reserve 4 drumsticks and 1 cup curry (without potatoes) for Chicken Biryani (see page 89) before serving.

Makes 4 to 6 servings

cuban pork sandwiches

- 1 pork loin roast (about 2 pounds)
- ½ cup orange juice
- 2 tablespoons lime juice
- 1 tablespoon minced garlic
- 1½ teaspoons salt
- ½ teaspoon crushed red pepper flakes
- 2 tablespoons yellow mustard
- 8 crusty bread rolls, split in half (6 inches each)
- 8 slices Swiss cheese
- 8 thin ham slices
- 4 small dill pickles, thinly sliced lengthwise

1. Coat **CROCK-POT**® slow cooker with nonstick cooking spray. Add pork loin.

2. Combine orange juice, lime juice, garlic, salt and pepper flakes in small bowl. Pour over pork. Cover; cook on LOW 7 to 8 hours or on HIGH 3½ to 4 hours. Transfer pork to cutting board and allow to cool. Cut into thin slices. If desired, reserve ¼ pork for Pork Tenderloin and Cabbage Salad with Chile Dressing (see page 93).

3. To serve, spread mustard on both sides of rolls. Divide pork slices among roll bottoms. Top with Swiss cheese slice, ham slice and pickle slices. Cover with top of roll.

4. Coat large skillet with nonstick cooking spray and heat over medium heat until hot. Working in batches, arrange sandwiches in skillet. Cover with foil and top with dinner plate to press down sandwiches.* (If necessary, weight with 2 to 3 cans to compress sandwiches lightly.) Heat until cheese is slightly melted, about 8 minutes. Serve immediately.
*Or use tabletop grill to compress and heat sandwiches.

Makes 8 servings

pork tenderloin and cabbage salad with chile dressing

4	to 6 ounces cooked pork tenderloin, sliced into strips (reserved from Cuban Pork Sandwiches, see page 92)
1½	cups finely shredded red cabbage
½	medium carrot, shredded
½	green onion, thinly sliced (green and white parts)
1½	tablespoons orange juice
1	tablespoons garlic chili sauce
½	tablespoon reduced-sodium soy sauce
⅛	teaspoon black pepper
1/16	teaspoon red pepper flakes

1. Combine pork, cabbage, carrot and green onion in large bowl. Toss gently but well.

2. Stir together juice, garlic chili sauce, soy sauce, black pepper and pepper flakes in small bowl. Pour over salad mixture. Toss gently but well.

Makes 2 (1⅓-cup) servings

tip
This salad tastes even better the next day.

ffamilysoccerhomeworkmomdinnerballetchoresdad
eakfast lessonsshoppingstudyingtra
otherworkfootballscrapbookingminivanscheduleda

DOUBLE DUTY

chipotle braised beef

- 3 pounds boneless chuck roast, cut into 2-inch pieces
- 1½ teaspoons salt, plus additional for seasoning
- ½ teaspoon ground black pepper, plus additional for seasoning
- 3 tablespoons vegetable oil, divided
- 1 large onion, cut into 1-inch dice (about 2½ cups)
- 2 red bell peppers, cut into 1-inch dice (about 3 cups)
- 1 tablespoon minced garlic
- 1 tablespoon chipotle chili powder
- 1 tablespoon paprika
- 1 teaspoon dried oregano
- 1 tablespoon ground cumin
- 3 tablespoons tomato paste
- 1 cup beef broth
- 1 can (about 14 ounces) diced tomatoes, drained
  Hot cooked rice (optional)

1. Pat beef dry with paper towels and season with salt and pepper. Heat 2 tablespoons oil in large skillet over medium-high heat. Working in batches, cook beef in skillet, turning to brown all sides. Transfer each batch to **CROCK-POT**® slow cooker as it is finished.

2. Add remaining 1 tablespoon oil to pan, reduce heat to medium and add onion. Cook, stirring occasionally, until just softened. Add bell peppers and cook 2 minutes. Stir in garlic, chili powder, paprika, oregano, cumin, tomato paste, 1½ teaspoon salt and ½ teaspoon pepper and cook 1 minute, stirring constantly. Transfer mixture to **CROCK-POT**® slow cooker. Return skillet to heat and add beef broth. Cook, stirring to scrape up any browned bits from the skillet. Pour over beef mixture. Stir in tomatoes. Cover and cook on LOW 7 hours, until beef is tender.

3. Skim fat from sauce. If desired, reserve 2 cups meat and 1½ cups sauce for Beef Enchiladas (see page 95). Serve over hot cooked rice, if desired.

Makes 4 to 6 servings

beef enchiladas

- 2 cups shredded cooked beef (reserved from Chipotle Braised Beef, see page 94)
- 2 cups shredded Mexican cheese blend, divided
- ½ cup frozen corn
- ½ cup rinsed and drained canned black beans
- ¼ cup chopped cilantro leaves
- 1½ cups sauce (reserved from Braised Chipotle Beef, see page 94)
- 1 can (10 ounces) diced tomatoes with green chilies, drained
- 12 (6-inch) corn tortillas
- 2 tablespoons vegetable oil
- ¼ cup thinly sliced green onions

1. Set oven rack in upper-middle position and preheat oven to 400°F. Coat 13 × 9-inch baking pan with nonstick cooking spray.

2. Combine cooked beef, 1¼ cups cheese, corn, beans and chopped cilantro in medium bowl, stirring to combine well; set aside.

3. Pulse reserved sauce and tomatoes with green chiles in food processor or blender until slightly chunky, about 10 pulses. Spread ¾ cup sauce evenly in prepared baking pan.

4. Brush both sides of 6 tortillas with oil and place in single layer (overlapping slightly if needed) on baking sheet. Warm in oven until softened, about 2 minutes. Spoon ⅓ cup beef mixture along center of each tortilla and roll up tightly. Place, seam side down, into prepared baking pan. Repeat with remaining tortillas and beef mixture, arranging side-by-side in pan. Spread tops with remaining sauce and sprinkle with remaining ¾ cup cheese. Cover pan with foil and bake until filling is heated through and cheese is melted, 20 minutes or until heated though. Remove foil and broil 2 minutes, until cheese is spotty brown. Top with green onions and serve immediately.

Makes 4 to 6 servings

japanese-style simmered chicken thighs

- 3 medium carrots, peeled and cut into 2-inch pieces
- ½ pound fresh shiitake mushrooms, stems removed, quartered
- 1 medium onion, cut into 1-inch dice
- 1 medium Japanese eggplant, halved lengthwise and cut into ½-inch-thick slices
- 2 pounds boneless, skinless chicken thighs
- ½ cup low-sodium soy sauce
- ⅓ cup chicken broth
- ⅓ cup sugar
- 1 tablespoon corn starch
- ¼ cup mirin
- 1 teaspoon grated fresh ginger
- 1 teaspoon minced garlic
- 1 star anise pod*
- 1 tablespoon sesame seeds, toasted

Hot cooked rice (optional)

*Or substitute ¼ teaspoon Chinese five-spice powder.

1. Place carrots, mushrooms, onion and eggplant in **CROCK-POT®** slow cooker. Top with chicken thighs; set aside.

2. Combine soy sauce, chicken broth, sugar, corn starch, mirin, ginger, garlic and star anise in small saucepan. Bring to simmer over medium heat, stirring occasionally, until sugar dissolves and mixture thickens slightly, 4 to 5 minutes. Pour over chicken and vegetables. Cover and cook on LOW about 7 hours or until chicken and vegetables are tender. Discard star anise. Serve over hot cooked rice, if desired. Stir in sesame seeds. If desired, reserve 4 chicken thighs, 1 cup vegetable mixture and ¾ cup sauce for Udon Chicken Soup (see page 97) before serving.

Makes 4 to 6 servings

udon chicken soup

- ¾ cup sauce (reserved from Japanese-Style Simmered Chicken Thighs, see page 96)
- 1 teaspoon toasted sesame oil
- 1 teaspoon Asian hot chile sauce
- 3¼ cups chicken broth
- 2 teaspoons rice vinegar
- 1 tablespoon low-sodium soy sauce
- 1 cup cooked mix vegetables (reserved from Japanese-Style Simmered Chicken Thighs, see page 96)
- 4 cooked chicken thighs (reserved from Japanese-Style Simmered Chicken Thighs, see page 96)
- ¾ pound bok choy, sliced crosswise ¼-inch thick
- ¼ cup thinly sliced green onions, plus more for garnish
- 2 packages (about 7 ounces each) refrigerated udon noodles*

*Or substitute 1 pound refrigerated fresh linguine or fettuccine noodles.

1. Fill medium saucepan half full with water and bring to a boil over high heat.

2. While water comes to a boil, combine reserved sauce, sesame oil, chile sauce, chicken broth, rice vinegar and soy sauce in large saucepan over medium-high heat. Bring to a boil. Add reserved vegetable mixture, chicken thighs and bok choy and simmer until chicken is warmed and bok choy is tender-crisp, 6 minutes. Stir in green onions.

3. Meanwhile, add udon noodles to boiling water and cook 2 to 3 minutes. Drain and divide evenly among 4 large soup bowls. Ladle 2 cups soup over each bowl of noodles and serve immediately, garnished with additional green onions, if desired.

Makes 4 servings

30-MINUTE MAIN DISHES

Hassle-free recipes
ready for your slow cooker
in half an hour or less

hoisin barbecue chicken thighs

⅔ cup hoisin sauce

⅓ cup ketchup

3 tablespoons quick-cooking tapioca

1 tablespoon sugar

1 tablespoon reduced-sodium soy sauce

¼ teaspoon crushed red pepper flakes

12 skinless, bone-in chicken thighs (about 3½ to 4 pounds)

Combine hoisin sauce, ketchup, tapioca, sugar, soy sauce and pepper flakes in **CROCK-POT®** slow cooker. Add chicken thighs, meat-side down. Cover and cook on LOW 8 to 9 hours. Spoon sauce over thighs to serve.

Makes 6 to 8 servings

gingered beef with peppers and mushrooms

1½ pounds boneless beef top round steak, cut into ¾-inch cubes

24 baby carrots

1 red bell pepper, seeded and chopped

1 green bell pepper, seeded and chopped

1 onion, chopped

1 package (8 ounces) fresh mushrooms, halved

2 tablespoons grated fresh ginger

1 cup lower-sodium beef broth

½ cup hoisin sauce

¼ cup quick-cooking tapioca

Hot cooked white rice (optional)

Combine beef, carrots, bell peppers, onion, mushrooms, ginger, beef broth, hoisin sauce and tapioca in **CROCK-POT®** slow cooker. Cover and cook on LOW 8 to 9 hours. Serve over white rice, if desired.

Makes 6 servings

chicken and wild rice casserole

- 2 slices bacon, chopped
- 3 tablespoons olive oil
- 1½ pounds chicken thighs, trimmed of excess skin
- ½ cup diced onion
- ½ cup diced celery
- 2 tablespoons Worcestershire sauce
- ¾ teaspoon salt
- ¼ teaspoon black pepper
- ½ teaspoon dried sage
- 1 cup converted long-grain white rice
- 1 package (4 ounces) wild rice
- 6 ounces brown mushrooms, wiped clean and quartered*
- 3 cups hot chicken broth, or enough to cover chicken
  Salt and black pepper, to taste
- 2 tablespoons chopped parsley, for garnish

*Use "baby bellas" or crimini mushrooms. Or, you may substitute white button mushrooms.

1. Microwave bacon on HIGH (100% power) 1 minute. Transfer to **CROCK-POT®** slow cooker. Add olive oil and spread evenly on bottom. Place chicken in **CROCK-POT®** slow cooker, skin side down. Add remaining ingredients in order given, except parsley. Cover; cook on LOW 3 to 4 hours or until rice is tender.

2. Uncover and let stand 15 minutes. Add salt and pepper, if desired. Remove skin before serving, if desired. Garnish with chopped parsley.

Makes 4 to 6 servings

easy cheesy bbq chicken

- 6 boneless, skinless chicken breasts (about 1½ pounds)
- 1 bottle (26 ounces) barbecue sauce
- 6 slices bacon
- 6 slices Swiss cheese

1. Place chicken in **CROCK-POT®** slow cooker. Cover with barbecue sauce. Cover; cook on LOW 8 to 9 hours. (If sauce becomes too thick during cooking, add a little water.)

2. Before serving, cut bacon slices in half. Cook bacon in microwave or on stove top, keeping bacon flat. Place 2 pieces cooked bacon on each chicken breast in **CROCK-POT®** slow cooker. Top with cheese. Cover; cook on HIGH until cheese melts.

Makes 6 servings

tip

To make cleanup easier, coat the inside of the **CROCK-POT®** slow cooker with nonstick cooking spray before adding the ingredients. To remove any sticky barbecue sauce residue, soak the stoneware in hot sudsy water, then scrub it with a plastic or nylon scrubber; don't use steel wool.

simple slow cooker pork roast

- 4 to 5 red potatoes, cut into bite-size pieces
- 4 carrots, cut into bite-size pieces
- 1 marinated pork loin roast* (3 to 4 pounds)
- ½ cup water
- 1 package (10 ounces) frozen baby peas

  Salt and black pepper, to taste

If marinated roast is unavailable, prepare marinade by mixing ¼ cup olive oil, 1 tablespoon minced garlic and 1½ tablespoons Italian seasoning. Place in large resealable plastic food storage bag with pork roast. Marinate in refrigerator at least 2 hours or overnight.

Place potatoes, carrots and pork roast in **CROCK-POT**® slow cooker. (If necessary, cut roast in half to fit.) Add water. Cover; cook on LOW 6 to 8 hours or until vegetables are tender. Add peas during last hour of cooking. Transfer pork to serving platter. Add salt and pepper, if desired. Slice and serve with vegetables.

Makes 6 servings

roast chicken with peas, prosciutto and cream

1 whole roasting chicken (about 2½ pounds), cut up

Salt and black pepper, to taste

5 ounces prosciutto, diced

1 small white onion, finely chopped

½ cup dry white wine

1 package (10 ounces) frozen peas

½ cup heavy cream

1½ tablespoons cornstarch

2 tablespoons water

4 cups farfalle pasta, cooked al dente

1. Season chicken pieces with salt and pepper. Combine chicken, prosciutto, onion and wine in **CROCK-POT®** slow cooker. Cover; cook on HIGH 3½ to 4 hours or on LOW 8 to 10 hours.

2. During last 30 minutes of cooking, add frozen peas and heavy cream to cooking liquid.

3. Remove chicken. Carve meat from bones and set aside on a warmed platter. Cover and keep warm.

4. Combine cornstarch and water. Add to cooking liquid in **CROCK-POT®** slow cooker. Cover; cook on HIGH 10 to 15 minutes or until thickened. To serve, spoon pasta onto individual plates. Place chicken on pasta and top each portion with sauce.

Makes 6 servings

roast ham with tangy mustard glaze

- 1 fully cooked boneless ham (about 3 pounds), visible fat removed
- ¼ cup packed dark brown sugar
- 2 tablespoons lemon juice, divided
- 1 tablespoon Dijon mustard
- ½ teaspoon ground allspice
- ¼ cup sugar
- 2 tablespoons cornstarch

1. Place ham in **CROCK-POT®** slow cooker. Combine brown sugar, 2 teaspoons lemon juice, mustard and allspice. Spoon evenly over ham. Cover; cook on LOW 6 to 7 hours or until ham is warm throughout and sauce is well absorbed. Transfer ham to warm serving platter.

2. Pour cooking liquid from **CROCK-POT®** slow cooker into small heavy saucepan. Add remaining lemon juice, sugar and cornstarch. Cook over medium-high heat until mixture boils. Reduce to medium heat. Cook and stir until sauce is thickened and glossy. Carve ham into slices and spoon sauce over individual servings.

Makes 12 to 15 servings

caribbean sweet potato and bean stew

- 2 medium sweet potatoes (about 1 pound), peeled and cut into 1-inch cubes
- 2 cups frozen cut green beans
- 1 can (15 ounces) black beans, rinsed and drained
- 1 can (14½ ounces) vegetable broth
- 1 small onion, sliced
- 2 teaspoons Caribbean jerk seasoning
- ½ teaspoon dried thyme
- ¼ teaspoon salt
- ¼ teaspoon ground cinnamon
- ⅓ cup slivered almonds, toasted*

To toast almonds, spread in single layer on baking sheet. Bake in preheated 350°F oven 8 to 10 minutes or until golden brown, stirring frequently.

Combine sweet potatoes, beans, broth, onion, jerk seasoning, thyme, salt and cinnamon in **CROCK-POT®** slow cooker. Cover; cook on LOW 5 to 6 hours or until vegetables are tender. Adjust seasonings. Serve with almonds.

Makes 4 servings

greek chicken and orzo

2 medium green bell peppers, cut into thin strips

1 cup chopped onion

2 teaspoons extra-virgin olive oil

8 chicken thighs, rinsed and patted dry

1 tablespoon dried oregano

½ teaspoon dried rosemary

½ teaspoon garlic powder

¾ teaspoon salt, divided

⅜ teaspoon black pepper, divided

8 ounces uncooked orzo pasta

Juice and grated peel of 1 medium lemon

½ cup water

2 ounces crumbled feta cheese (optional)

Chopped fresh parsley (optional)

tip

Browning skin-on chicken not only adds flavor and color, but also prevents the skin from shrinking and curling during the long, slow cooking process.

1. Coat **CROCK-POT®** slow cooker with nonstick cooking spray. Add bell peppers and onion.

2. Heat oil in large skillet over medium-high heat until hot. Brown chicken on both sides. Transfer to **CROCK-POT®** slow cooker, overlapping slightly if necessary. Sprinkle chicken with oregano, rosemary, garlic powder, ¼ teaspoon salt and ⅛ teaspoon black pepper. Cover; cook on LOW 5 to 6 hours, on HIGH 3 to 4 hours or until chicken is tender.

3. Transfer chicken to separate plate. Turn **CROCK-POT®** slow cooker to HIGH. Stir orzo, lemon juice, lemon peel, water and remaining ½ teaspoon salt and ¼ teaspoon black pepper into **CROCK-POT®** slow cooker. Top with chicken. Cover; cook 30 minutes or until pasta is done. Garnish with feta cheese and parsley, if desired.

Makes 4 servings

simple shredded pork tacos

- 2 pounds boneless pork roast
- 1 cup salsa
- 1 can (4 ounces) chopped green chiles
- ½ teaspoon garlic salt
- ½ teaspoon black pepper

  Flour or corn tortillas

  Optional toppings: salsa, sour cream, diced tomatoes, shredded cheese, shredded lettuce

1. Place roast, salsa, chiles, garlic salt and pepper in **CROCK-POT**® slow cooker. Cover; cook on LOW 8 hours or until meat is tender.

2. Remove pork from **CROCK-POT**® slow cooker; shred with 2 forks. Serve on flour tortillas with sauce. Top as desired.

Makes 6 servings

nice 'n' easy italian chicken

- 4 boneless, skinless chicken breasts (about 1 pound)
- 8 ounces mushrooms, sliced
- 1 medium green bell pepper, chopped
- 1 medium zucchini, diced
- 1 medium onion, chopped
- 1 jar (26 ounces) pasta sauce

  Hot cooked linguini or spaghetti

Combine all ingredients except pasta in **CROCK-POT®** slow cooker. Cover; cook on LOW 6 to 8 hours or until chicken is tender. Serve over linguini.

Makes 4 servings

smoky chipotle cassoulet

- 1 pound boneless, skinless chicken thighs, cubed
- 1 teaspoon salt
- 1 teaspoon ground cumin
- 1 bay leaf
- 1 chipotle pepper in adobo sauce, minced
- 1 medium onion, diced
- 1 can (15 ounces) navy beans, rinsed and drained
- 1 can (15 ounces) black beans, rinsed and drained
- 1 can (14½ ounces) crushed tomatoes, undrained
- 1½ cups chicken stock
- ½ cup fresh-squeezed orange juice
- ¼ cup chopped fresh cilantro (optional)

1. Combine all ingredients except cilantro in **CROCK-POT®** slow cooker. Cover; cook on LOW 7 to 8 hours or on HIGH 4 to 5 hours.

2. Remove bay leaf before serving. Garnish with cilantro, if desired.

Makes 6 servings

knockwurst and cabbage

Olive oil

8 to 10 knockwurst sausages

1 head red cabbage, cut into ¼-inch slices

½ cup thinly sliced white onion

2 teaspoons caraway seeds

1 teaspoon salt

4 cups chicken broth

1. Heat oil in skillet over medium heat until hot. Brown knockwursts on all sides, turning as they brown. Transfer to **CROCK-POT®** slow cooker.

2. Add cabbage and onion to **CROCK-POT®** slow cooker. Sprinkle with caraway seeds and salt. Add broth. Cover; cook on LOW 4 hours, on HIGH about 2 hours or until knockwursts are cooked through and cabbage and onions are soft.

Makes 8 servings

mango spiced ribs

- 2 tablespoons vegetable oil
- 3 pounds beef short ribs
- 1 cup mango chutney
- 1 teaspoon curry powder
- ½ teaspoon salt
- ½ teaspoon ground cinnamon
- 1 clove garlic, minced

1. Heat oil in skillet over medium heat until hot. Brown ribs on all sides, turning as they brown. Remove from pan and set aside to cool slightly.

2. Combine chutney, curry powder, salt, cinnamon and garlic. Rub mixture into ribs. Place in **CROCK-POT®** slow cooker. Drizzle remaining chutney mixture over ribs. Cover; cook on LOW 6 to 8 hours or on HIGH 3 to 4 hours.

Makes 6 servings

mushroom barley stew

1 tablespoon olive oil

1 medium onion, finely chopped

1 cup chopped carrots (about 2 carrots)

1 clove garlic, minced

1 cup uncooked pearl barley

1 cup dried wild mushrooms, broken into pieces

1 teaspoon salt

½ teaspoon black pepper

½ teaspoon dried thyme

5 cups vegetable broth

1. Heat oil in medium skillet over medium-high heat. Add onion, carrots and garlic; cook and stir 5 minutes or until tender. Place in **CROCK-POT®** slow cooker.

2. Add barley, mushrooms, salt, pepper and thyme. Stir in broth. Cover; cook on LOW 6 to 7 hours. Adjust seasonings.

Makes 4 to 6 servings

tip

To turn this thick robust stew into a soup, add 2 to 3 additional cups of broth. Cook the same length of time.

beef roast with dark rum sauce

- 1 teaspoon ground allspice
- ½ teaspoon salt
- ½ teaspoon black pepper
- ¼ teaspoon ground cloves
- 1 beef rump roast (about 3 pounds)
- 2 tablespoons extra-virgin olive oil
- 1 cup dark rum, divided
- ½ cup beef broth
- 2 cloves garlic, minced
- 2 whole bay leaves, broken in half
- ½ cup packed dark brown sugar
- ¼ cup lime juice

1. In a small bowl, combine allspice, salt, pepper and cloves. Rub spices onto all sides of roast.

2. Heat oil in skillet over medium heat until hot. Sear beef on all sides, turning as it browns. Transfer to **CROCK-POT®** slow cooker. Add ½ cup rum, broth, garlic and bay leaves. Cover; cook on LOW 1 hour.

3. In a small bowl, combine remaining ½ cup rum, brown sugar and lime juice, stirring well. Pour over roast. Continue cooking on LOW 4 to 6 hours or until beef is fork-tender.

4. Remove and slice roast. Spoon sauce over beef to serve.

Makes 6 servings

SOUP FOR SUPPER

Make a meal of a steamy bowl
of one of these hearty, satisfying soups

hearty chicken tequila soup

- 1 small onion, cut into 8 wedges
- 1 cup frozen corn, thawed
- 1 can (14½ ounces) diced tomatoes with mild green chilies, undrained
- 2 cloves garlic, minced
- 2 tablespoons chopped fresh cilantro, plus additional for garnish
- 1 whole fryer chicken (about 3½ pounds)
- 2 cups chicken broth
- 3 tablespoons tequila
- ¼ cup sour cream

1. Spread onions on bottom of **CROCK-POT®** slow cooker. Add corn, tomatoes, garlic and 2 tablespoons cilantro. Mix well to combine. Place chicken on top of tomato mixture.

2. Pour broth and tequila over chicken and tomato mixture. Cover; cook on LOW 8 to 10 hours.

3. Transfer chicken to cutting board. Remove skin and bones. Pull meat apart with 2 forks into bite-size pieces. Return chicken to **CROCK-POT®** slow cooker and stir.

4. Serve with dollop of sour cream and garnish with cilantro.

Makes 2 to 4 servings

italian hillside garden soup

- 1 tablespoon extra-virgin olive oil
- 1 cup chopped green bell pepper
- 1 cup chopped onion
- ½ cup sliced celery
- 1 can (14½ ounces) diced tomatoes with basil, garlic and oregano, undrained
- 1 can (15½ ounces) navy beans, drained and rinsed
- 1 medium zucchini, chopped
- 1 cup frozen cut green beans, thawed
- 2 cans (14 ounces each) chicken broth
- ¼ teaspoon garlic powder
- 1 package (9 ounces) refrigerated sausage- or cheese-filled tortellini pasta
- 3 tablespoons chopped fresh basil

  Grated Asiago or Parmesan cheese (optional)

1. Heat oil in large skillet over medium-high heat until hot. Add bell pepper, onion and celery. Cook and stir 4 minutes or until onions are translucent. Transfer to **CROCK-POT®** slow cooker.

2. Add tomatoes with juice, navy beans, zucchini, green beans, broth and garlic powder. Cover; cook on LOW 7 hours or on HIGH 3½ hours.

3. Turn **CROCK-POT®** slow cooker to HIGH. Add tortellini and cook 20 to 25 minutes longer or until pasta is tender. Stir in basil. Garnish each serving with cheese.

Makes 6 servings

tip

Can't find refrigerated tortellini? Substitute 1 package (about 12 ounces) frozen tortellini or ravioli. Cook frozen pasta for 30 minutes or until tender but firm.

lentil soup with ham and bacon

- 8 ounces chopped bacon
- 8 cups beef broth
- 1½ pounds dried lentils
- 2 cups chopped ham
- 1 cup chopped carrots
- ¾ cup chopped celery
- ¾ cup chopped tomatoes
- ½ cup chopped onion
- 2 teaspoons salt
- 2 teaspoons black pepper
- ½ teaspoon dried marjoram

1. Heat skillet over medium heat until hot. Add bacon. Cook and stir until crisp. Transfer to **CROCK-POT®** slow cooker using slotted spoon.

2. Add remaining ingredients. Cover; cook on LOW 8 to 10 hours or on HIGH 6 to 8 hours or until lentils are tender.

Makes 8 servings

country sausage and bean soup

- 2 cans (14 ounces each) chicken broth
- 1½ cups hot water
- 1 cup dried black beans, sorted and rinsed
- 1 cup chopped onion
- 2 bay leaves
- 1 teaspoon sugar
- ⅛ teaspoon ground red pepper
- 6 ounces reduced-fat country pork sausage
- 1 cup chopped tomato
- 1 tablespoon Worcestershire sauce
- 2 teaspoons extra-virgin olive oil
- 1 tablespoon chili powder
- 1½ teaspoons ground cumin
- ½ teaspoon salt
- ¼ cup chopped cilantro

1. Combine broth, water, beans, onions, bay leaves, sugar and red pepper in **CROCK-POT®** slow cooker. Cover; cook on LOW 8 hours or on HIGH 4 hours.

2. Coat large skillet with nonstick cooking spray. Heat over medium-high heat until hot. Add sausage and cook until beginning to brown, stirring to break up meat.

3. Add sausage and remaining ingredients, except cilantro, to **CROCK-POT®** slow cooker. Cover; cook on HIGH 15 minutes to blend flavors. To serve, sprinkle with cilantro.

Makes 9 servings

smoked sausage and navy bean soup

8 cups chicken broth

1 pound dried navy beans, sorted and rinsed

2 ham hocks (about 1 pound total)

2 cloves garlic, minced

2 onions, diced

1 cup diced carrots

1 cup diced celery

1 can (14½ ounces) diced tomatoes, undrained

2 tablespoons tomato paste

1 bay leaf

1 teaspoon dried thyme

1 beef smoked sausage (16 ounces), cut into ½-inch rounds

1. Place broth in large saucepan. Heat over medium-high heat until broth begins to boil. Cover and reduce heat to LOW.

2. Place beans in **CROCK-POT®** slow cooker. Add remaining ingredients, except broth and sausage. Carefully pour in hot broth. Cover; cook on HIGH 8 to 9 hours or until beans are tender.

3. Remove bay leaf. Remove ham hocks from **CROCK-POT®** slow cooker, and let stand until cool enough to handle. Remove ham from hocks, chop and add back to **CROCK-POT®** slow cooker. Stir in sausage. Cover; cook on HIGH 15 to 30 minutes longer or until sausage is heated through.

Makes 8 servings

nana's mini meatball soup

- 1 pound ground beef
- 1 pound ground pork
- 1½ cups finely grated Pecorino Romano or Parmesan cheese
- 1 cup Italian bread crumbs
- 2 eggs
- 1 bunch flat-leaf parsley
  Kosher salt and black pepper
- 3 quarts chicken stock
- 1 bunch escarole, coarsely chopped
- ½ box (about 8 ounces) ditalini pasta, cooked

1. Combine beef, pork, cheese, bread crumbs, eggs, parsley, salt and pepper in large bowl. Mix well by hand and roll into ¾-inch meatballs.

2. Add meatballs and chicken stock to **CROCK-POT**® slow cooker. Cook on LOW 9 hours or on HIGH 5 hours.

3. Add escarole and cook until escarole has wilted and is bright green and tender, about 15 minutes. Add cooked ditalini to soup and serve.

Makes 6 to 8 servings

tip
Substitute spinach for escarole, if desired.

sweet and sour moroccan lamb soup

- 3 tablespoons olive oil
- 1 pound boneless lamb shoulder, cut into thin strips, fat removed
- 1 teaspoon peeled and grated ginger
- ½ teaspoon ground turmeric
- 1 can (28 ounces) peeled plum tomatoes, drained
- 7 cups cold water
- 1 large onion, chopped
- 1 bunch fresh cilantro, stemmed, ¼ cup loosely packed reserved for garnish
  Kosher salt and black pepper
- 1 cup orzo, cooked
- 2 tablespoons lemon juice
- ½ teaspoon ground cinnamon
- 1 cup dates, finely chopped

1. Heat olive oil in heavy pan over medium-high to high heat. Sear lamb on all sides.

2. Transfer lamb to **CROCK-POT®** slow cooker and add ginger, turmeric, tomatoes, water, onion, cilantro, salt and pepper. Cover and cook on LOW 12 hours or on HIGH 8 hours.

3. Add cooked orzo, lemon juice and cinnamon. Taste and adjust seasonings. Ladle into serving bowls and garnish with chopped dates.

Makes 4 to 6 servings

northwoods smoked ham and bean soup

. . . .

- 2 tablespoons olive oil
- 2 large onions, chopped
- 6 cloves garlic, peeled and minced
- 6 cups chicken stock
- 2 smoked ham hocks
- 2 cups cubed cooked smoked ham
- 1 can (28 ounces) whole peeled plum tomatoes, drained and coarsely chopped
- 1 bunch fresh parsley, stemmed and chopped
- 4 sprigs fresh thyme
- 4 bay leaves
- 2 cans (15 ounces each) cannellini beans, drained and rinsed
- ½ pound cooked orecchiette, cavatelli or ditalini pasta
  Kosher salt and black pepper

1. Heat olive oil in skillet over medium heat. Add onions and cook, stirring occasionally, until soft and fragrant, about 10 minutes. Add garlic and cook 1 minute.

2. Place onion and garlic mixture, stock, ham hocks, ham, tomatoes, parsley, thyme and bay leaves in **CROCK-POT®** slow cooker. Cook on LOW 10 hours or on HIGH 6 hours.

3. Stir in beans and pasta and continue to cook on HIGH until heated through.

4. Season to taste with salt and pepper and serve.

Makes 6 to 8 servings

italian beef and barley soup

- 1 boneless beef top sirloin steak (about 1½ pounds)
- 1 tablespoon vegetable oil
- 4 medium carrots or parsnips, cut into ¼-inch slices
- 1 cup chopped onion
- 1 teaspoon dried thyme
- ½ teaspoon dried rosemary
- ¼ teaspoon black pepper
- ⅓ cup uncooked pearl barley
- 2 cans (about 14 ounces each) beef broth
- 1 can (about 14 ounces) diced tomatoes with Italian seasoning, undrained

1. Cut beef into 1-inch pieces. Heat oil over medium-high heat in large skillet. Brown beef on all sides; set aside.

2. Place carrots and onion in **CROCK-POT**® slow cooker; sprinkle with thyme, rosemary and pepper. Top with barley and beef. Pour broth and tomatoes over meat.

3. Cover; cook on LOW 8 to 10 hours or until beef is tender.

Makes 6 servings

tip

Use pearl barley, not quick-cooking barley, because it will stand up better to long cooking.

beef, lentil and onion soup

. . . .

     Nonstick cooking spray

¾ pound beef for stew (1-inch pieces)

2 cups chopped carrots

1 cup sliced celery

1 cup uncooked lentils

2 teaspoons dried thyme

¼ teaspoon black pepper

⅛ teaspoon salt

3¼ cups water

1 can (10½ ounces) condensed French onion soup, undiluted

. . . .

1. Spray large skillet with cooking spray. Heat skillet over medium-high heat. Add beef; cook until browned on all sides.

2. Place carrots, celery and lentils in **CROCK-POT®** slow cooker. Top with beef. Sprinkle with thyme, pepper and salt. Pour water and soup over mixture. Cover; cook on LOW 7 to 8 hours or on HIGH 3½ to 4 hours or until meat and lentils are tender.

Makes 4 servings

mushroom soup

- 2 tablespoons olive oil
- 2 large Vidalia onions, coarsely chopped
- 1 package (10 ounces) cremini mushrooms
- 1 package (10 ounces) button mushrooms
  Kosher salt and black pepper
- 2 tablespoons butter
- 6 to 10 cloves garlic, peeled and coarsely chopped
- 2 tablespoons sherry
- 4 cups beef or vegetable stock

1. Heat olive oil in large skillet over medium-high heat. Add onions and mushrooms and season well with salt and pepper. Cook vegetables, stirring often, until cooked down and fragrant, about 8 to 10 minutes.

2. Add butter and garlic and cook gently another 1 to 2 minutes. Add sherry to pan and stir to scrape up any bits stuck to bottom.

3. Transfer sherry and vegetables into **CROCK-POT**® slow cooker and add stock. Cover and cook on LOW 5 to 6 hours or on HIGH 3 to 4 hours.

Makes 4 to 6 servings

note

Mushroom soup is often made with beef stock because the deep flavor of the mushrooms balances perfectly with a hearty stock, but this recipe can be an easy vegetarian main dish simply by using vegetable stock instead.

chicken and wild rice soup

- 3 cans (14½ ounces each) chicken broth
- 1 pound boneless, skinless chicken breasts or thighs, cut into bite-size pieces
- 2 cups water
- 1 cup sliced celery
- 1 cup diced carrots
- 1 package (6 ounces) converted long-grain and wild rice mix with seasoning packet
- ½ cup chopped onion
- ½ teaspoon black pepper
- 2 teaspoons white vinegar (optional)
- 1 tablespoon dried parsley

1. Combine broth, chicken, water, celery, carrots, rice and seasoning packet, onion and pepper in **CROCK-POT®** slow cooker; mix well.

2. Cover; cook on LOW 6 to 7 hours or on HIGH 4 to 5 hours or until chicken is tender.

3. Stir in vinegar, if desired. Sprinkle with parsley before serving.

Makes 9 servings

tortilla soup

- 2 cans (about 14 ounces each) chicken broth
- 1 can (about 14 ounces) diced tomatoes with green chilies
- 2 cups chopped carrots
- 2 cups frozen corn, thawed
- 1½ cups chopped onions
- 1 can (8 ounces) tomato sauce
- 1 tablespoon chili powder
- 1 teaspoon ground cumin
- ¼ teaspoon garlic powder
- 2 cups chopped cooked chicken (optional)

serving suggestion

Top with shredded Monterey Jack cheese or crushed tortilla chips.

1. Combine broth, tomatoes, carrots, corn, onions, tomato sauce, chili powder, cumin and garlic powder in **CROCK-POT®** slow cooker. Cover; cook on LOW 6 to 8 hours.

2. Stir in chicken, if desired. Ladle into bowls. Top each serving with cheese and tortilla chips.

Makes 6 servings

chuck and stout soup

- -

- 2 tablespoons olive oil
- 3 pounds beef chuck, cut into 1-inch cubes
  Kosher salt and black pepper
- 8 cups beef stock
- 3 large onions, thinly sliced
- 3 stalks celery, diced
- 6 carrots, peeled and diced
- 4 cloves garlic, peeled and minced
- 2 packages (10 ounces each) cremini mushrooms, thinly sliced
- 1 package (about 1 ounce) dried porcini mushrooms, processed to a fine powder
- 4 sprigs fresh thyme
- 1 bottle (12 ounces) stout beer
  Flat-leaf parsley to garnish

- -

1. Heat oil in skillet over medium-high to high heat. Season meat with salt and pepper. In two batches, brown beef on all sides, taking care to not crowd meat. Meanwhile, in large saucepan, bring beef stock to a boil and reduce by half.

2. Remove beef and place in **CROCK-POT®** slow cooker. Add reduced stock and all remaining ingredients except parsley. Cover and cook on LOW 10 hours or on HIGH 6 hours.

3. Garnish with parsley and serve.

Makes 6 to 8 servings

note

A coffee grinder works best for processing dried mushrooms, but a food processor or blender can also be used.

ffamilysoccerhomeworkmomdinnerballetchoresdad
eakfast...lessonsshoppingstudyin
otherworkfootballscrapbookingminivanscheduleda

winter's best bean soup

- 6 ounces bacon, diced
- 10 cups chicken broth
- 3 cans (about 15 ounces each) Great Northern beans, drained
- 1 can (about 14 ounces) diced tomatoes, undrained
- 1 large onion, chopped
- 1 package (10 ounces) frozen sliced or diced carrots
- 2 teaspoons bottled minced garlic
- 1 fresh rosemary sprig or 1 teaspoon dried rosemary
- 1 teaspoon black pepper

1. Cook bacon in medium skillet over medium-high heat until just cooked; drain and transfer to **CROCK-POT®** slow cooker. Add remaining ingredients.

2. Cover; cook on LOW 8 hours or until beans are tender. Remove rosemary sprig. Mince leaves and add to soup before serving.

Makes 8 to 10 servings

serving suggestion

Place slices of toasted Italian bread in bottom of individual soup bowls. Drizzle with olive oil. Pour soup over bread and serve.

split pea soup with andouille sausage

1½ pounds smoked andouille sausage, sliced thin

1 onion, chopped

1 stalk celery, finely chopped

2 cloves garlic, minced

1 pound split peas, picked over

4 cups chicken stock

4 cups water

½ teaspoon dried thyme

1 bay leaf

2 carrots, peeled and diced

Salt and black pepper

Croutons or crusty bread

1. Brown sausage in heavy skillet over medium heat. Using a slotted spoon, transfer to paper towels to drain, and pour off all but 1 tablespoon fat from skillet.

2. Add onion, celery and garlic to skillet and cook over medium heat, stirring frequently, until celery is softened. Place sausage, onion, celery and garlic in **CROCK-POT®** slow cooker. Add split peas, stock, water, thyme, bay leaf and carrots. Cover and cook on LOW 7 to 9 hours or on HIGH 4 to 5 hours or until carrots are tender.

3. Discard bay leaf, season soup with salt and pepper and serve with croutons or bread.

Makes 6 to 8 servings

tip

Drizzle finished soup with an aged balsamic vinegar or top with shredded sharp Cheddar cheese, if desired.

FAMILY FAVORITES

Your weeknight dinner dilemmas
are easily solved with these recipes
sure to please the whole family

meatless sloppy joes

2 cups thinly sliced onions

2 cups chopped green bell peppers

1 can (about 15 ounces) kidney beans, drained and mashed

1 can (8 ounces) tomato sauce

2 tablespoons ketchup

1 tablespoon yellow mustard

2 cloves garlic, finely chopped

1 teaspoon chili powder

   Cider vinegar (optional)

4 sandwich rolls

Combine onions, bell peppers, beans, tomato sauce, ketchup, mustard, garlic and chili powder in **CROCK-POT**® slow cooker. Cover; cook on LOW 5 to 5½ hours or until vegetables are tender. Season to taste with cider vinegar, if desired. Serve on rolls.

Makes 4 servings

meatballs and spaghetti sauce

Meatballs

2 pounds 90% lean ground beef

1 cup bread crumbs

1 onion, chopped

2 eggs, beaten

¼ cup minced flat-leaf parsley

2 teaspoons minced garlic

½ teaspoon dry mustard

½ teaspoon black pepper

Olive oil

Spaghetti Sauce

1 can (28 ounces) peeled whole tomatoes

½ cup chopped fresh basil

2 tablespoons olive oil

2 cloves garlic (or more to taste), finely minced

1 teaspoon sugar

Salt and black pepper, to taste

Cooked spaghetti

> **tip**
>
> Recipe can be doubled for a 5-, 6- or 7-quart CROCK-POT® slow cooker.

1. Combine all meatball ingredients except oil. Form into walnut-sized balls. Heat oil in skillet over medium heat until hot. Sear meatballs on all sides, turning as they brown. Transfer to **CROCK-POT®** slow cooker.

2. Combine all sauce ingredients in medium bowl. Pour over meatballs, stirring to coat. Cover; cook on LOW 3 to 5 hours or on HIGH 2 to 4 hours.

3. Adjust seasonings, if desired. Serve over spaghetti.

Makes 6 to 8 servings

turkey with chunky cherry relish

- 1 bag (16 ounces) frozen dark cherries, coarsely chopped
- 1 can (about 14 ounces) diced tomatoes with green chilies
- 1 package (6 ounces) dried cherry-flavored cranberries or dried cherries, coarsely chopped
- 2 small onions, thinly sliced
- 1 small green bell pepper, chopped
- ½ cup packed brown sugar
- 2 tablespoons quick-cooking tapioca
- 1½ tablespoons salt
- ½ teaspoon ground cinnamon
- ½ teaspoon black pepper
- 1 bone-in turkey breast (about 2½ to 3 pounds)
- 2 tablespoons water
- 1 tablespoon cornstarch

1. Place cherries, tomatoes, cranberries, onions, bell pepper, brown sugar, tapioca, salt, cinnamon and black pepper in **CROCK-POT®** slow cooker; mix well.

2. Place turkey on top of mixture. Cover; cook on LOW 7 to 8 hours or until temperature registers over 170°F on meat thermometer inserted into thickest part of breast, not touching bone. Remove turkey from **CROCK-POT®** slow cooker; keep warm.

3. Increase temperature to HIGH. Combine water and cornstarch in small bowl to form smooth paste. Stir into cherry mixture. Cook, uncovered, on HIGH 15 minutes or until sauce is thickened. Adjust seasonings, if desired. Slice turkey and top with relish.

Makes 4 to 6 servings

corned beef & cabbage

2 onions, thickly sliced

1 corned beef (about 3 pounds) with seasoning packet

1 package (8 to 10 ounces) baby carrots

6 medium potatoes, peeled and cut into wedges

1 cup water

3 to 5 slices bacon

1 head green cabbage, cut into wedges

1. Layer onion slices to cover bottom of **CROCK-POT®** slow cooker. Add corned beef with seasoning packet, carrots and potato wedges. Pour 1 cup water over. Cover and cook on LOW 10 hours.

2. With 30 minutes left in cooking time, heat large saucepan over medium-high heat. Add bacon; cook and stir until bacon is crisp. Remove bacon with slotted spoon and drain on paper towels. When cool enough to handle, crumble bacon.

3. Place cabbage in saucepan with bacon drippings, cover with water. Bring to a boil and cook 20 to 30 minutes or until cabbage in tender. Drain.

4. Serve corned beef with vegetables. Top with crumbled bacon.

Makes 6 servings

macaroni and cheese

- 6 cups cooked macaroni
- 2 tablespoons butter
- 4 cups evaporated milk
- 6 cups (24 ounces) shredded Cheddar cheese
- 2 teaspoons salt
- ½ teaspoon black pepper

In large mixing bowl, toss macaroni with butter. Stir in evaporated milk, cheese, salt and pepper; place in **CROCK-POT**® slow cooker. Cover; cook on HIGH 2 to 3 hours.

Makes 6 to 8 servings

tip

Make this mac 'n' cheese recipe more fun. Add some tasty mix-ins: diced green or red bell pepper, peas, hot dog slices, chopped tomato, browned ground beef or chopped onion. Be creative!

classic chili

- 1½ pounds ground beef
- 1½ cups chopped onion
- 1 cup chopped green bell pepper
- 2 cloves garlic, minced
- 3 cans (15 ounces each) dark red kidney beans, rinsed and drained
- 2 cans (15 ounces each) tomato sauce
- 1 can (14½ ounces) diced tomatoes, undrained
- 2 to 3 teaspoons chili powder
- 1 to 2 teaspoons dry hot mustard
- ¾ teaspoon dried basil
- ½ teaspoon black pepper
- 1 to 2 dried hot chili peppers (optional)

1. Cook and stir ground beef, onion, bell pepper and garlic in large skillet until meat is browned and onion is tender. Drain fat and discard. Transfer mixture to **CROCK-POT®** slow cooker.

2. Add beans, tomato sauce, tomatoes with juice, chili powder, mustard, basil, black pepper and chili peppers, if desired; mix well. Cover; cook on LOW 8 to 10 hours or on HIGH 4 to 5 hours.

3. If used, remove chili peppers before serving.

Makes 6 servings

chicken and rice

- 3 cans (10¾ ounces each) condensed cream of chicken soup, undiluted
- 2 cups uncooked instant rice
- 1 cup water
- 1 pound boneless, skinless chicken breasts or chicken breast tenders
- ½ teaspoon salt
- ¼ teaspoon black pepper
- ¼ teaspoon paprika
- ½ cup diced celery

Combine soup, rice and water in **CROCK-POT**® slow cooker. Add chicken; sprinkle with salt, pepper and paprika. Sprinkle celery over chicken. Cover; cook on LOW 6 to 8 hours or on HIGH 3 to 4 hours.

Makes 4 servings

entfamilysoccerhomeworkmomdinnerballetchoresda
eakfas...essonsshoppingstudyi
brotherworkfootballscrapbookingminivanscheduleda

FAMILY FAVORITES

pizza soup

2   cans (14½ ounces each) stewed tomatoes with Italian seasonings, undrained

2   cups beef broth

1   cup sliced mushrooms

1   small onion, chopped

1   tablespoon tomato paste

¼   teaspoon salt, or to taste

¼   teaspoon black pepper, or to taste

½   pound turkey Italian sausage, casings removed

    Shredded mozzarella cheese

1. Combine tomatoes with juice, broth, mushrooms, onion, tomato paste, salt and pepper in **CROCK-POT®** slow cooker.

2. Shape sausage into marble-size balls. Gently stir into soup mixture. Cover; cook on LOW 6 to 7 hours. Adjust salt and pepper, if necessary. Serve with cheese.

Makes 4 servings

sweet and sour chicken

- ¼ cup chicken broth
- 2 tablespoons low-sodium soy sauce
- 2 tablespoons hoisin sauce
- 1 tablespoon cider vinegar
- 1 tablespoon tomato paste
- 2 teaspoons packed brown sugar
- 1 garlic clove, minced
- ¼ teaspoon black pepper
- 1 pound boneless, skinless chicken thighs, cut into 1-inch pieces
- 2 teaspoons cornstarch
- 2 tablespoons minced chives
- Hot cooked rice

1. Combine broth, soy sauce, hoisin sauce, vinegar, tomato paste, brown sugar, garlic and pepper in **CROCK-POT**® slow cooker. Stir well to mix.

2. Add chicken thighs, and stir well to coat. Cover; cook on LOW 2½ to 3½ hours.

3. Remove chicken with slotted spoon and keep warm. Combine cornstarch and 2 tablespoons cooking liquid in small bowl. Add to **CROCK-POT**® slow cooker. Stir in chives. Turn heat to HIGH. Stir 2 minutes or until sauce is slightly thickened. Serve chicken and sauce over rice.

Makes 4 servings

chicken with italian sausage

- 10 ounces bulk mild or hot Italian sausage
- 6 boneless, skinless chicken thighs
- 1 can (about 15 ounces) white beans, rinsed and drained
- 1 can (about 15 ounces) red beans, rinsed and drained
- 1 cup chicken broth
- 1 medium onion, chopped
- 1 teaspoon black pepper
- ½ teaspoon salt
- Chopped fresh parsley

1. Brown sausage in large skillet over medium-high heat, stirring to break up meat. Drain fat and discard. Spoon sausage into **CROCK-POT**® slow cooker.

2. Trim fat from chicken and discard. Place chicken, beans, broth, onion, pepper and salt in **CROCK-POT**® slow cooker. Cover; cook on LOW 5 to 6 hours.

3. Adjust seasonings, if desired. Slice each chicken thigh on the diagonal. Serve with sausage and beans. Garnish with parsley.

Makes 6 servings

enffamilysoccerhomeworkmomdinnerballetchoresda
reakfas lessonsshoppingstudyi
rotherworkfootballscrapbookingminivanscheduleda

easy family burritos

- 1 boneless beef chuck shoulder roast (2 to 3 pounds)
- 1 jar (24 ounces) or 2 jars (16 ounces each) salsa

  Flour tortillas, warmed

  Optional toppings: shredded cheese, sour cream, salsa, shredded lettuce, diced tomato, diced onion or guacamole

1. Place roast in **CROCK-POT®** slow cooker; top with salsa. Cover; cook on LOW 8 to 10 hours.

2. Remove beef from **CROCK-POT®** slow cooker. Shred beef with 2 forks. Return to cooking liquid and mix well. Cover; cook 1 to 2 hours longer or until heated through.

3. Serve shredded beef wrapped in warm tortillas. Top as desired.

Makes 8 servings

matzo ball soup

- 3 quarts (12 cups) chicken stock
- 4 parsnips, peeled and sliced into ½-inch rounds
- 2 carrots, peeled and sliced into ½-inch rounds
- 3 leeks, sliced
- 1 large onion, sliced
- 1 small rotisserie chicken, cooked (optional)
- 1 tablespoon fresh dill
  Matzo Balls (recipe follows)
  Kosher salt and black pepper

1. Add stock to **CROCK-POT®** slow cooker. Add parsnips, carrots, leeks and onion to stock and cook on LOW 8 to 10 hours or on HIGH 4 to 5 hours.

2. Remove skin and bones from chicken and cut into bite-sized pieces. Add chicken, if desired, dill and Matzo Balls to hot soup and cook on HIGH until heated through. Season to taste with salt and pepper and serve.

Makes 4 to 6 servings

matzo balls

- 4 large eggs
- 5 tablespoons butter or margarine, melted
- 1 small bunch flat-leaf parsley, minced
- 1 tablespoon minced fresh sage
- 1¼ cups matzo meal
- ½ cup water
  Salt and black pepper

1. Combine all ingredients in mixing bowl and blend with fork, making sure to generously season mixture with salt and pepper. Roll into golf ball-size or smaller matzo balls.

2. Cover and place in refrigerator 30 to 60 minutes.

3. Bring a pot of salted water to boil over medium-high heat. Drop matzo balls in and simmer 20 minutes. Remove with a slotted spoon and reserve until needed.

mushroom-beef stew

- 1 **pound beef stew meat**
- 1 **can (10¾ ounces) condensed cream of mushroom soup, undiluted**
- 2 **cans (4 ounces each) sliced mushrooms, drained**
- 1 **package (1 ounce) dry onion soup mix**
  Hot cooked noodles

Combine all ingredients except noodles in **CROCK-POT®** slow cooker. Cover; cook on LOW 8 to 10 hours. Serve over noodles.

Makes 4 servings

note

Button mushrooms are the most common mushrooms grown and sold. They are plump and dome-shaped with a smooth texture and mild flavor. The color of button mushrooms varies from white to pale tan.

three-bean turkey chili

- 1 pound lean ground turkey
- 1 small onion, chopped
- 1 can (28 ounces) diced tomatoes, undrained
- 1 can (15 ounces) chickpeas, rinsed and drained
- 1 can (15 ounces) kidney beans, rinsed and drained
- 1 can (15 ounces) black beans, rinsed and drained
- 1 can (8 ounces) tomato sauce
- 1 can (4 ounces) diced mild green chiles
- 1 to 2 tablespoons chili powder

1. Cook and stir turkey and onion in medium nonstick skillet over medium-high heat until turkey is no longer pink. Drain and discard fat. Transfer to **CROCK-POT®** slow cooker.

2. Add remaining ingredients; mix well. Cover; cook on HIGH 6 to 8 hours.

Makes 6 to 8 servings

bbq beef sandwiches

- 1 boneless beef chuck roast (about 3 pounds)
- ¼ cup ketchup
- 2 tablespoons brown sugar
- 2 tablespoons red wine vinegar
- 1 tablespoon Dijon mustard
- 1 tablespoon Worcestershire sauce
- 1 clove garlic, crushed
- ¼ teaspoon salt
- ¼ teaspoon liquid smoke
- ⅛ teaspoon black pepper
- 10 to 12 French rolls or sandwich buns, sliced in half

1. Place beef in **CROCK-POT®** slow cooker. Combine remaining ingredients, except rolls, in medium bowl; pour over meat. Cover; cook on LOW 8 to 9 hours.

2. Remove beef from **CROCK-POT®** slow cooker; shred with 2 forks.

3. Combine beef with 1 cup sauce from **CROCK-POT®** slow cooker. Evenly distribute meat and sauce mixture among warmed rolls.

Makes 10 to 12 servings

tip

To reduce the amount of fat in the **CROCK-POT®** slow cooker meals, trim and discard excess fat from meats, or choose lean cuts.

like grandma's chicken 'n' dumplings

- 2 cups cooked chicken
- 1 can (10¾ ounces) condensed cream of mushroom soup, undiluted
- 1 can (10¾ ounces) condensed cream of chicken soup, undiluted
- 2 soup cans water
- 4 teaspoons all-purpose flour
- 2 teaspoons chicken bouillon granules
- ½ teaspoon black pepper
- 1 can refrigerated buttermilk biscuits (8 biscuits)

1. Mix all ingredients except biscuits in **CROCK-POT®** slow cooker.

2. Cut biscuits into quarters and gently stir into mixture. Cover; cook on LOW 4 to 6 hours.

Makes 4 to 6 servings

tip

Don't add water to the **CROCK-POT®** slow cooker, unless the recipe specifically says to do so. Foods don't lose as much moisture during slow cooking as they can during conventional cooking, so follow the recipe guidelines for best results.

Your slow cooker can make family dinner
any night of the week a little sweeter
with these hands-free dessert ideas

s'mores fondue

- 1 pound milk chocolate, chopped
- 2 jars (7 ounces each) marshmallow cream
- ⅔ cup half-and-half
- 2 teaspoons vanilla
  Mini marshmallows (optional)
  Assorted cookies, graham crackers and candies
  Fresh fruit such as apples, bananas and strawberries, peeled and sliced or cut into 1-inch pieces as necessary

1. Combine chocolate, marshmallow cream, half-and-half and vanilla in **CROCK-POT®** slow cooker. Cover and cook on LOW 1½ to 3 hours, stirring once after 1 hour.

2. Garnish top of fondue dip with mini marshmallows, if desired, and serve with assorted cookies, graham crackers, candies and fruit for dipping.

Makes 8 to 12 servings

glazed orange poppy seed cake

. . . .

Batter

- 1½ cups biscuit baking mix
- ¾ cup granulated sugar
- 2 tablespoons poppy seeds
- ½ cup sour cream
- 1 egg
- 2 tablespoons milk
- 1 teaspoon vanilla
- 2 teaspoons orange zest

Glaze

- ¼ cup orange juice
- 2 cups powdered sugar, sifted
- 2 teaspoons poppy seeds

. . . .

1. Coat inside of 4-quart **CROCK-POT®** slow cooker with nonstick cooking spray. Cut waxed paper circle to fit bottom of **CROCK-POT®** slow cooker (trace insert bottom and cut slightly smaller to fit). Spray lightly with cooking spray.

2. Whisk together baking mix, granulated sugar and poppy seeds in medium bowl; set aside. In another bowl, blend sour cream, egg, milk, vanilla and orange zest. Whisk wet ingredients into dry mixture until thoroughly blended.

3. Spoon batter into prepared **CROCK-POT®** slow cooker and smooth top. Place paper towel under lid, then cover. Cook on HIGH 1½ hours. (Cake is done when top is no longer shiny and a toothpick inserted in center comes out clean.)

4. Invert cake onto cooling rack, peel off waxed paper and allow to cool (right side up) on cooling rack.

5. Whisk orange juice into powdered sugar. Cut cake into 8 wedges and place on cooling rack with a tray underneath to catch drips. With a small spatula or knife, spread glaze over top and cut sides of each wedge. Sprinkle poppy seeds over wedges and allow glaze to set.

Makes 8 servings

faml**ysoccerhomeworkmom**dinner**balletchoresdad**
eakfast**lessonsshoppingstudying**
otherworkfootballscrapbookingminivanscheduled

SWEET TREATS

strawberry rhubarb crisp

Fruit

- **4** cups sliced hulled strawberries
- **4** cups diced rhubarb (about 5 stalks), cut into ½-inch dice
- **1½** cups granulated sugar
- **2** tablespoons lemon juice
- **1½** tablespoons cornstarch, plus water (optional)

Topping

- **1** cup all-purpose flour
- **1** cup old-fashioned oats
- **½** cup granulated sugar
- **½** cup packed brown sugar
- **½** teaspoon ground ginger
- **½** teaspoon ground nutmeg
- **½** cup butter (1 stick), cut into pieces
- **½** cup sliced almonds, toasted*

To toast almonds, spread in single layer on baking sheet. Bake in preheated 350°F oven 8 to 10 minutes or until golden brown, stirring frequently.

1. Prepare fruit. Coat **CROCK-POT**® slow cooker with nonstick cooking spray. Place strawberries, rhubarb, granulated sugar and lemon juice in **CROCK-POT**® slow cooker and mix well. Cook on HIGH 1½ hours or until fruit is tender.

2. If fruit is dry after cooking, add a little water. If fruit has too much liquid, mix cornstarch with a small amount of water and stir into fruit. Cook on HIGH an additional 15 minutes or until cooking liquid is thickened.

3. Preheat oven to 375°F. Prepare topping. Combine flour, oats, sugars, ginger and nutmeg in medium bowl. Cut in butter using pastry cutter or 2 knives until mixture resembles coarse crumbs. Stir in almonds.

4. Remove lid from **CROCK-POT**® slow cooker and gently sprinkle topping onto fruit. Transfer stoneware to oven. Bake 15 to 20 minutes or until topping begins to brown.

Makes 8 servings

fresh berry compote

- 2 cups fresh blueberries
- 4 cups fresh sliced strawberries
- 2 tablespoons orange juice
- ½ to ¾ cup sugar
- 4 slices (½ × 1½ inches) lemon peel with no white pith
- 1 cinnamon stick or ½ teaspoon ground cinnamon

1. Place blueberries in **CROCK-POT®** slow cooker. Cover; cook on HIGH 45 minutes until blueberries begin to soften.

2. Add strawberries, orange juice, ½ cup sugar, lemon peel and cinnamon stick. Stir to blend. Cover; cook on HIGH 1 to 1½ hours or until berries soften and sugar dissolves. Check for sweetness and add more sugar if necessary, cooking until added sugar dissolves.

3. Remove insert from **CROCK-POT®** slow cooker to heatproof surface and let cool. Serve compote warm or chilled.

Makes 4 servings

tip

To turn this compote into a fresh-fruit topping for cake, ice cream, waffles or pancakes, carefully spoon out fruit, leaving cooking liquid in **CROCK-POT®** slow cooker. Blend 1 to 2 tablespoons cornstarch with ¼ cup cold water until smooth. Add to cooking liquid and cook on HIGH until thickened. Return fruit to sauce and blend in gently.

entfamilysoccerhomeworkmomdinnerballetchoresda
breakfast lessonsshoppingstudyingtr
protherworkfootballscrapbookingminivanscheduledar

SWEET TREATS

red hot applesauce

10 to 12 apples, peeled, cored and chopped

¾ cup hot cinnamon candies

½ cup apple juice or water

Combine apples, candies and apple juice in the **CROCK-POT®** slow cooker. Cover; cook on LOW 7 to 8 hours or on HIGH 4 hours or until desired consistency. Serve warm or chilled.

Makes 6 servings

fudge and cream pudding cake

- 2 tablespoons unsalted butter
- 1 cup all-purpose flour
- ¾ cup packed light brown sugar
- 5 tablespoons unsweetened cocoa powder, divided
- 2 teaspoons baking powder
- ½ teaspoon ground cinnamon
- ⅛ teaspoon salt
- 1 cup light cream
- 1 tablespoon vegetable oil
- 1 teaspoon vanilla
- ¾ cup packed dark brown sugar
- 1¾ cups hot water
- Whipped cream or ice cream (optional)

1. Coat inside of 4½-quart **CROCK-POT®** slow cooker with butter. Combine flour, light brown sugar, 3 tablespoons cocoa, baking powder, cinnamon and salt in medium bowl. Add cream, oil and vanilla; stir well to combine. Pour batter into **CROCK-POT®** slow cooker.

2. Combine dark brown sugar and remaining 2 tablespoons cocoa in medium bowl. Add hot water; stir well to combine. Pour sauce over cake batter. Do not stir. Cover; cook on HIGH 2 hours.

3. Spoon portions of pudding cake onto plates. Serve with whipped cream, if desired.

Makes 8 to 10 servings

streusel pound cake

- 1 package (16 ounces) pound cake mix, plus ingredients to prepare mix
- ¼ cup packed light brown sugar
- 1 tablespoon all-purpose flour
- ¼ cup chopped nuts
- 1 teaspoon ground cinnamon

  Strawberries, blueberries, raspberries and/or powdered sugar (optional)

Coat 4½-quart **CROCK-POT®** slow cooker with nonstick cooking spray. Prepare cake mix according to package directions; stir in brown sugar, flour, nuts and cinnamon. Pour batter into **CROCK-POT®** slow cooker. Cover; cook on HIGH 1½ to 1¾ hours or until toothpick inserted into center of cake comes out clean. Serve with berries and powdered sugar, if desired.

Makes 6 to 8 servings

ntfamilysoccerhomeworkmomdinnerballetchoresda
eakfast lessonsshoppingstudyingtr
otherworkfootballscrapbookingminivanscheduleda

SWEET TREATS

classic baked apples

- ¼ cup packed dark brown sugar
- 2 tablespoons golden raisins
- 1 teaspoon grated lemon peel
- 6 small to medium baking apples, washed and cored
- 1 teaspoon ground cinnamon
- 2 tablespoons butter, cut into small pieces
- ¼ cup orange juice
- ¼ cup water
- Whipped cream (optional)

1. Combine brown sugar, raisins and lemon peel in small bowl. Fill core of each apple with mixture. Place apples in **CROCK-POT®** slow cooker. Sprinkle with cinnamon and dot with butter. Pour orange juice and water over apples. Cover; cook on LOW 7 to 9 hours or on HIGH 2½ to 3½ hours.

2. To serve, place apples in individual bowls. Top with sauce. Garnish with whipped cream, if desired.

Makes 4 servings

mexican chocolate bread pudding

- 1½ cups light cream
- 4 ounces unsweetened chocolate, coarsely chopped
- 2 eggs, beaten
- ½ cup sugar
- ¾ teaspoon ground cinnamon
- ½ teaspoon ground allspice
- 1 teaspoon vanilla
- ⅛ teaspoon salt
- ½ cup currants
- 3 cups Hawaiian-style sweet bread, challah or rich egg bread, cut into ½-inch cubes

  Whipped cream (optional)

  Chopped macadamia nuts (optional)

1. Heat cream in large saucepan. Add chocolate and stir until chocolate melts.

2. Combine eggs, sugar, cinnamon, allspice, vanilla and salt in medium bowl. Stir in currants. Add to chocolate mixture. Stir well to combine. Pour into **CROCK-POT®** slow cooker.

3. Gently fold in bread cubes using plastic spatula. Cover; cook on HIGH 3 to 4 hours or until a knife inserted near center comes out clean.

4. Serve warm or chilled. If desired, top with generous dollop of whipped cream and sprinkling of nuts.

Makes 6 to 8 servings

ntfamilysoccerhomeworkmomdinnerballetchoresdad
reakfast lessonsshoppingstudying
rotherworkfootballscrapbookingminivanscheduled

SWEET TREATS

cinn-sational swirl cake

- 1 box (21½ ounces) cinnamon swirl cake mix
- 1 cup sour cream
- 1 cup cinnamon-flavored baking chips
- 1 cup water
- ¾ cup vegetable oil
- 1 package (4-serving size) instant French vanilla pudding and pie filling mix
  Cinnamon ice cream (optional)

1. Coat 4½-quart **CROCK-POT®** slow cooker with nonstick cooking spray. Set cinnamon swirl mix packet aside. Place remaining cake mix in **CROCK-POT®** slow cooker.

2. Add sour cream, cinnamon chips, water and oil; stir well to combine. Batter will be slightly lumpy. Add reserved cinnamon swirl mix, slowly swirling through batter with knife. Cover; cook on LOW 3 to 4 hours or on HIGH 1½ to 1¾ hours or until toothpick inserted into center of cake comes out clean.

3. Serve warm with cinnamon ice cream, if desired.

Makes 10 to 12 servings

triple chocolate fantasy

- 2 pounds white almond bark, broken into pieces
- 1 bar (4 ounces) sweetened chocolate, broken into pieces*
- 1 package (12 ounces) semisweet chocolate chips
- 3 cups lightly toasted, coarsely chopped pecans**

*Use your favorite high-quality chocolate candy bar

**To toast pecans, spread in single layer on baking sheet. Bake in preheated 350°F oven 8 to 10 minutes or until golden brown, stirring frequently.

1. Place bark, sweetened chocolate and chocolate chips in **CROCK-POT®** slow cooker. Cover; cook on HIGH 1 hour. Do not stir.

2. Turn slow cooker to LOW. Continue cooking 1 hour, stirring every 15 minutes. Stir in nuts.

3. Drop mixture by tablespoonfuls onto baking sheet covered with waxed paper; let cool. Store in tightly covered container.

Makes 36 pieces

variations

Here are a few ideas for other imaginative items to add in along with or instead of pecans: raisins, crushed peppermint candy, candy-coated baking bits, crushed toffee, peanuts or pistachios, chopped gum drops, chopped dried fruit, candied cherries, chopped marshmallows or sweetened coconut.

hawaiian fruit compote

- 3 cups coarsely chopped fresh pineapple
- 3 grapefruits, peeled and sectioned
- 2 cups chopped fresh peaches
- 2 to 3 limes, peeled and sectioned
- 1 mango, peeled and chopped
- 2 bananas, peeled and sliced
- 1 tablespoon lemon juice
- 1 can (21 ounces) cherry pie filling
- Slivered almonds (optional)

1. Place all ingredients except almonds in **CROCK-POT**® slow cooker and toss lightly. Cover; cook on LOW 4 to 5 hours or on HIGH 2 to 3 hours.

2. Serve with almonds, if desired.

Makes 6 to 8 servings

serving suggestion

Try warm, fruity compote in place of maple syrup on your favorite pancakes or waffles for a great way to start your day. This sauce is also delicious served over roasted turkey, pork roast or baked ham.

familysoccerhomeworkmomdinnerballetchoresdad
reakfast essonsshoppingstudying
rotherworkfootballscrapbookingminivanscheduledan

SWEET TREATS

easy chocolate pudding cake

. . . .

1   package (6-serving size) instant chocolate pudding and pie filling mix

3   cups milk

1   package (about 18 ounces) chocolate fudge cake mix, plus ingredients to prepare mix

Crushed peppermint candies (optional)

Whipped topping or ice cream (optional)

1. Coat 4-quart **CROCK-POT®** slow cooker with nonstick cooking spray. Place pudding mix in **CROCK-POT®** slow cooker. Whisk in milk.

2. Prepare cake mix according to package directions. Carefully pour cake mix into **CROCK-POT®** slow cooker. Do not stir. Cover; cook on HIGH 1½ hours or until cake tester inserted into center comes out clean.

3. Spoon into cup or onto plate; serve warm with crushed peppermint candies and whipped topping, if desired.

Makes 16 servings

tip

Allow breads, cakes and puddings to cool at least 5 minutes before scooping or removing them from the **CROCK-POT®** stoneware.

spicy fruit dessert

- ¼ cup orange marmalade
- ¼ teaspoon pumpkin pie spice
- 1 can (6 ounces) frozen orange juice concentrate
- 2 cups canned pears, drained and diced
- 2 cups carambola (star fruit), sliced and seeds removed

1. Combine marmalade, pumpkin pie spice, orange juice concentrate, pears and carambola in the **CROCK-POT**® slow cooker.

2. Cover; cook on LOW 4 to 6 hours or on HIGH 2 to 3 hours or until done. Serve warm over pound cake or ice cream.

Makes 4 to 6 servings

SWEET TREATS

cherry delight

- 1 can (21 ounces) cherry pie filling
- 1 package (18¼ ounces) yellow cake mix
- ½ cup (1 stick) butter, melted
- ⅓ cup chopped walnuts

Whipped topping or vanilla ice cream (optional)

Place pie filling in **CROCK-POT®** slow cooker. Mix together cake mix and butter in medium bowl. Spread evenly over cherry filling. Sprinkle walnuts on top. Cover; cook on LOW 3 to 4 hours or on HIGH 1½ to 2 hours. Spoon into serving dishes and serve warm with whipped topping or ice cream, if desired.

Makes 8 to 10 servings

caravan and apple pound cake

- 4 medium baking apples, cored, peeled and cut into wedges
- ½ cup apple juice
- ½ pound caramels, unwrapped
- ¼ cup creamy peanut butter
- 1½ teaspoons vanilla
- ½ teaspoon ground cinnamon
- ⅛ teaspoon ground cardamom
- 1 prepared pound cake, sliced

1. Coat inside of **CROCK-POT**® slow cooker with nonstick cooking spray. Layer apples, apple juice and caramels in **CROCK-POT**® slow cooker.

2. Mix together peanut butter, vanilla, cinnamon and cardamom in small bowl. Drop by teaspoons onto apples. Cover; cook on LOW 6 to 8 hours or on HIGH 3 to 4 hours.

3. Stir thoroughly, and cook 1 hour longer. To serve, spoon warm over cake slices.

Makes 6 to 8 servings

INDEX

METRIC CHART

VOLUME MEASUREMENTS (dry)

1/8 teaspoon = 0.5 mL
1/4 teaspoon = 1 mL
1/2 teaspoon = 2 mL
3/4 teaspoon = 4 mL
1 teaspoon = 5 mL
1 tablespoon = 15 mL
2 tablespoons = 30 mL
1/4 cup = 60 mL
1/3 cup = 75 mL
1/2 cup = 125 mL
2/3 cup = 150 mL
3/4 cup = 175 mL
1 cup = 250 mL
2 cups = 1 pint = 500 mL
3 cups = 750 mL
4 cups = 1 quart = 1 L

VOLUME MEASUREMENTS (fluid)

1 fluid ounce (2 tablespoons) = 30 mL
4 fluid ounces (1/2 cup) = 125 mL
8 fluid ounces (1 cup) = 250 mL
12 fluid ounces (1 1/2 cups) = 375 mL
16 fluid ounces (2 cups) = 500 mL

WEIGHTS (mass)

1/2 ounce = 15 g
1 ounce = 30 g
3 ounces = 90 g
4 ounces = 120 g
8 ounces = 225 g
10 ounces = 285 g
12 ounces = 360 g
16 ounces = 1 pound = 450 g

DIMENSIONS

1/16 inch = 2 mm
1/8 inch = 3 mm
1/4 inch = 6 mm
1/2 inch = 1.5 cm
3/4 inch = 2 cm
1 inch = 2.5 cm

OVEN TEMPERATURES

250°F = 120°C
275°F = 140°C
300°F = 150°C
325°F = 160°C
350°F = 180°C
375°F = 190°C
400°F = 200°C
425°F = 220°C
450°F = 230°C

BAKING PAN AND DISH EQUIVALENTS

Utensil	Size in Inches	Size in Centimeters	Volume	Metric Volume
Baking or Cake Pan (square or rectangular)	8×8×2	20×20×5	8 cups	2 L
	9×9×2	23×23×5	10 cups	2.5 L
	13×9×2	33×23×5	12 cups	3 L
Loaf Pan	8½×4½×2½	21×11×6	6 cups	1.5 L
	9×9×3	23×13×7	8 cups	2 L
Round Layer Cake Pan	8×1½	20×4	4 cups	1 L
	9×1½	23×4	5 cups	1.25 L
Pie Plate	8×1½	20×4	4 cups	1 L
	9×1½	23×4	5 cups	1.25 L
Baking Dish or Casserole			1 quart/4 cups	1 L
			1½ quart/6 cups	1.5 L
			2 quart/8 cups	2 L
			3 quart/12 cups	3 L